To Ponna Bass on her 14th Birthday
J. Russell

Marie Antoinette

Marie Antoinette

MARIE ANTOINETTE

BY BERNARDINE KIELTY

Illustrated by DOUGLAS GORSLINE

RANDOM HOUSE · NEW YORK

Published in New York by Random House, Inc. and simultaneously in Toronto, Canada by Random House of Canada Limited
Library of Congress Catalog Card Number: 55-10011

Manufactured in the United States of America

Contents

Marie Antoinette

1

Happy Princess

Marie Antoinette was one of the most captivating princesses of all time. With her high-combed blonde headdress and her lightly billowing costume of frothy blue, she was like a china figure of exquisite workmanship—a creature light-hearted and gay, out of a faraway golden age.

That shimmering age through which she stepped so merrily has now gone forever. In the short span of Marie Antoinette's lifetime an old world died and a new world was born. There is little doubt that all of us are better off and happier now because of that vast eruption of human spirit that brought about the French Revolution and banished the gilded monarchs. That old world deserved to go because it was built up on selfishness and injustice. But the people living through it could not see ahead. To the downtrodden the Revolution meant freedom; to those born in palaces it spelled tragedy.

Marie Antoinette was caught in the whirling center of revolutionary fury because it was her fate to be born into a royal family, to be born in the middle of the eighteenth century, to be born in the powerful country of Austria.

Antoine was the name by which Marie Antoinette was called during the happy childhood days in Austria. She was a pretty little girl in a lace-paper blue-and-white valentine sort of way. Her hair was pale blonde and her clear white skin was luminous—so everyone who saw her tells us; her eyes were like the sky and her cheeks were bright with health. Maybe her lips were a trifle too thick for great beauty. She laughed a little too loud, and perhaps too much. But she was young and alive, and the world was in her hand.

Antoine was an archduchess, as was every Austrian

princess. Her mother was Queen Maria Theresa, one of the most famous women rulers in history, and her father was the Emperor Francis I, not so famous, but beloved by his wife and children. Maria Theresa and Francis had sixteen children, of whom Marie Antoinette (Antoine) was the fifteenth. There were eleven girls and five boys.

These were the Hapsburgs, the most important royal family of Europe at the time into which we are now looking—the middle of the eighteenth century. They had reigned in splendor for five centuries, and now they assumed their right to rule to be God-given. They loved their subjects—the millions of people who did the work, plowed the fields and built the houses and dug the mines; the shepherds on the mountains; the fishermen on the Danube River; the soldiers and the sailors. But no Hapsburg ever dreamed of questioning his own and his family's superiority over all of these. It is superfluous even to mention it now, so remote from their minds and from the minds of their people as well was any notion of the idea of human equality.

But we are getting away from Antoine, so bright and shining. She was born Maria Antonia Anna Josepha Joanna, in old Vienna on November 2, 1755. This was All Souls' Day, the day dedicated by the Church to those who are dead—a grim day on which to be born. Looking back two hundred years as we are, we doubtless read meanings and portents where none were. But fate seemed to cast a cloud over Marie Antoinette from the day of her birth. Only now, from this distance, can we see how the ominous cloud spread and spread until it covered her completely.

On the very day that she was born a catastrophic earthquake followed by a great fire shook the land of Portugal and destroyed the capital, Lisbon. Thirty thousand people were killed and the King and Queen of Portugal, who were to be the godparents of little Marie Antoinette, were unable to journey to Vienna for the baptismal celebration.

None the less Vienna rejoiced in the birth of still another princess. The people were given two days' holiday, and there was dancing in the streets.

The Vienna home of the Hapsburgs was the Hofburg palace. But the castle where little Antoine spent most of her childhood was Schönbrunn. It goes without saying that castles are big and that most of them are forbidding. Schönbrunn had 1,440 rooms with 129 kitchens. Big, yes! But not forbidding. The castle still stands, rather simple for its great size, not too far from the center of Vienna. In the days when Antoine played there, a lovely park stretched out like a green tapestry to set off the castle's noble whiteness. Deer roamed the deep woods, and the children's dogs scampered after squirrels.

In this stately home with its high-ceilinged rooms and its well-kept garden paths, the children of Maria Theresa and the Emperor Francis grew up in a friendly sort of way. Sometimes the whole family—those parts of it which were walking at the time and didn't have to be wheeled—would go out together for a promenade. This would most likely be on a Sunday afternoon when the people of Vienna would also be taking their ease. Everyone loved to see the royal family strolling, the smaller children taking the hands of their older brothers and sisters, Maria Theresa and Francis smiling graciously toward all they passed.

But this was not an entirely true picture of that enormous and very important household. The father, as seen out walking on a Sunday afternoon, was in his own role. He liked to gather his children around him. He particularly loved little Marie Antoinette, his youngest. But Maria Theresa was far too busy to find time to be a mother. She was a public character, a great queen, one of the most powerful women in the world. She maneuvered wars and made treaties between nations. For years she kept all Europe in a turmoil for what she thought to be the good of her own country and her own family. She had a remarkable aptitude for matters political. She was sensible and shrewd, and for the most part understood the men with whom she had to deal. But she was not a wise mother.

The family walks made a pleasing picture for the people of Vienna. Also, when an important figure from some foreign court visited Vienna, Maria Theresa again called her children to circle round her as for a photograph. It was a good photograph indeed for the foreign emissary to carry back in words to his sovereign—of a

The little archduchesses danced and played together

good woman who not only ruled a country but brought up her family in the tenderest home traditions.

As facts stand, however, no mother of a prospective movie starlet could have sacrificed her children's welfare for ambition more than Maria Theresa sacrificed her daughters. Particularly the welfare of her youngest and prettiest daughter, Antoine. History has no story of neglect that has dug deeper into tragedy. The daughters of Maria Theresa and the Emperor Francis were destined, almost all of them, to be queens, yet they were allowed to grow up uneducated and almost illiterate. They were spoiled, they were given a false set of values, they were entirely unprepared—even in a practical way—for their destinies.

Antoine and Caroline, the two little archduchesses nearest in age, were brought up together for twelve years and were the closest of friends. They played in the park with their dogs; they walked sedately with their beloved governess, Countess Brandeiss; they avoided their oldest brother, Joseph, because he liked to scold them.

Every day and all day they were at someone's beck and call. Maids, footmen, nurses as well as governesses, surrounded them and their sisters and brothers. Real freedom—to run in and out as they pleased, even to walk into a village street—they never knew. But within the limitations of castle life, experience had already taught them how to avoid what was most unpleasant and how best to do what they pleased. Antoine in particular insinuated herself into the hearts of the older people around her. She could ward off an order with a hug or kiss; she was charming; and no one could say her nay.

From nurse to governess to tutor, Marie Antoinette passed almost unscathed as to school work and discipline. Kind and indulgent Countess Brandeiss gave her and Caroline their lessons and did what she could to make them easy and agreeable. If word came, as it did from time to time, to show a sample of the children's work to Maria Theresa, the governess would first trace out the letters in pencil and let Antoine and Caroline write over them. The consequence was that Antoine's handwriting remained childish and unformed even after she was grown up and married and gone away from Austria forever.

On special occasions little Antoine spoke in Latin. This was to impress the visitors at court. But Countess Brandeiss helped her learn the words by heart and she had no idea what they meant.

The tutor who came to her when she was thirteen found that she could not spell, that she knew practically no history, even of her own country, no geography whatsoever, and that she despised reading. She never did learn to spell properly, and all her life she continued to dislike reading. "A distaste for reading," Maria Theresa once said, "is common to nearly all my children."

Antoine loved music, though she never learned to

play an instrument. One of the greatest of all musical geniuses was living at the same time in Vienna—a child nearly her own age. That was little Wolfgang Amadeus Mozart. When Mozart was seven he was invited to court to play the harpsichord for the great Empress Maria Theresa. Antoine was eight at the time, but so far as anyone knows she did not hear him, then or ever. What a joyous experience it would have been if the young Mozart had played for the little archduchesses in one of the gold-and-white Schönbrunn music rooms! And then gone out to run with them in the park!

Maria Theresa could have done this so easily. She could have done so much for her children! But actually she did so little! She was too busy. Up at five in the morning, she worked at her country's affairs for twelve hours, then gave the rest of her time to the social life of the court with its parties and balls and dinners. This was the part her husband, the Emperor, thoroughly enjoyed. For he was a light-hearted man who did not take the business of government too seriously.

The children were only one of the many departments to be attended to on Maria Theresa's agenda. Every hour of their day was planned. Maria Theresa demanded and received full reports on their activities. All that was missing in her scheme of being a good mother was her own physical presence: the only thing she didn't see fit to give her children (besides education) was her time and herself. Oftentimes she didn't see them for a week or ten days.

The court physician, Dr. Van Sweiten, was ordered to visit the children every day and report to the mother. If a child was sick, Maria Theresa flew to the bedside. Sickness was something she could deal with in a practical way, and she was a practical woman. But she recognized only the obvious diseases—measles, mumps, smallpox. With nerves or a general weakness, she had no sympathy. A child who was nervous or pale or weak or tired was disobedient, to Maria Theresa's way of thinking, or at best, disagreeable.

"It is my wish that the children eat everything set before them without making any objections. They are not to make any remarks about preferring this or that, or to discuss their food. . . . Though Joanna has a repulsion against fish (Joanna was one of Antoine's slightly older sisters) no one is to give way to her in this matter. . . . All my children seem to have an aversion against fish, but they must all overcome this. There is to be no relenting."

Poor Joanna! She was one of the frail neurotic ones. She died in 1762 at the age of twelve.

Joanna died of smallpox. Although an inoculation against smallpox had been discovered, Maria Theresa, who disapproved of anything new, did not permit its use. Consequently death stalked her court. Seven of her family caught the disease, and four of them died, among them Charles, her favorite son. In this day of vaccinations it is hard for us to realize the terrors of such a scourge.

When Maria Theresa did see her children, she was never very mother-like. She ordered them to kiss her hand at certain times and on definite occasions. Little Antoine threw her arms about her beloved Brandeiss, but not about her mother.

Between Antoine and her father, the Emperor, however, there was a bond of warm affection. It may be that her light-heartedness came to her from him, and that her lack of seriousness was due to heredity as well as to her upbringing. Emperor Francis was not brilliant. He was a gentleman and a prince. He was gay and handsome, and Vienna under his influence became the city of charm and vivacious gaiety which it was to remain for another hundred years. But when he married Maria Theresa, it has been said, he could scarcely read and write. It was she who put the crown of Emperor on his head by making him co-regent, and though she loved him dearly, she never let him forget.

The Emperor enjoyed all his children but the spiritual bond between him and Antoine went very deep.

When Leopold, the second son, was to be married to the Spanish Infanta, the Emperor and Maria Theresa prepared to go to Innsbruck where the ceremony was to be held. They were already seated in the carriage and the Emperor had said his usual lengthy affectionate farewells to the children. The young archdukes stood respectfully beside the carriage, waiting for it to start, but the little girls had already returned to the castle.

"Call Antoine back!" cried the Emperor as if impelled by some force outside himself. "I must see that child again!"

To Maria Theresa it was all foolishness. She was already impatient with the long-drawn farewells. An affair of state was ahead of them, and playful goodbyes seemed to her a self-indulgence.

But Antoine was called and now came running like a little whirlwind.

Her father caught her up and held her close for a long minute. "My dear one!" Then he kissed her twice, once on each cheek in the Austrian way, and put her down.

At last the carriage started on its way.

As long as she could see it Antoine waved her hand, and the Emperor turned around and waved back.

It was Antoine's last view of her father. He was taken ill during the wedding festivities at Innsbruck, and died there on August 18, 1765.

Antoine never forgot her father. But she was only ten when he died, and in such a large family children are born, sisters and brothers get sick, some among them die. Even a father goes away. But childhood itself swings merrily along. A little girl of ten is never sad for long.

So Marie Antoinette (little Antoine) grew up in innocence, with no education to check her, like a bird in a cage. Freedom was hers only in seconds, but in these seconds she fluttered in anticipation. Later—when she was free indeed—she misused her liberty. Her mother had a fund of common sense but she ruled her children so firmly that it was wrung out of them. She thought for them. All they need do was obey, or evade obeying, but never did they have the incentive to think things out for themselves. All that Marie Antoinette was taught—and she was taught that strictly—was (1) the divinity of royalty, and (2) unbounded devotion to Austria, to the Hapsburgs, and to Maria Theresa.

2

Betrothal

During the third week of April, 1770, Vienna—that gay light-hearted city—was the scene of sparkling festivity. The Emperor, who was now Joseph, oldest brother of Antoine, gave a reception and ball for 3,000 guests at Belvedere, high up on the mountainside overlooking the city. On the following night the French ambassador entertained at a great banquet. The avenues were lighted with torches, the trees in the palace gardens twinkled with lanterns, and dazzling fireworks were shot into the darkness. Maria Theresa received the congratulations of all the foreign ambassadors and their suites.

The climax of the week was April 19th when at six o'clock in the evening all the great nobles of Austria assembled at the ancient gray Church of the Augustines. At the end of the long procession walked the Empress, leading her youngest daughter to the altar. This was of course Antoine, who from this day on was to be known as Marie Antoinette. She wore a shining gown of cloth-of-silver that reached to the floor, with a long train carried by two of the ladies-in-waiting of the court. Solemnly she knelt down beside her brother Ferdinand, the Archduke Ferdinand, who was there to take the place of the Dauphin of France. The Pope's ambassador gave his blessing. And cannon and musketry thundered the news to the world.

This was the marriage day of little Antoine, aged fourteen, to the Dauphin of France. Marie Antoinette was now officially the Dauphiness, and Maria Theresa was seeing a dream come true.

To understand why this marriage was so important to the Empress, we must take a glance at what was happening in Europe at this time, in the middle of the eighteenth century.

We must look particularly at France.

Antoine was married by proxy to the French Dauphin

France and Austria, the two most powerful nations in Europe, had been enemies for two hundred years. The Hapsburg family ruled not only Austria but Spain and the Low Countries as well. This meant that France had enemies both on the south and the north. So Louis XIV—famous king of France for more than fifty years through the seventeenth century—undertook to oust the Hapsburgs, at least on the south. Under his leadership France won and the Hapsburgs were put out of Spain forever. The Bourbons, the ruling house of France, then took their place.

But it was not simple. The price of victory for France was high. She had weakened Austria, yes, but in doing so she had strengthened Prussia. Prussia at that time was a fresh young country along the Baltic Sea ruled by a king who was vigorous and ruthless and a near-genius. This was Frederick II, now known to us as Frederick the Great. He had become an ally of France, but as an ally had already proven himself thoroughly unreliable. Treaties meant little to Frederick, and he was about as dangerous a friend as an enemy.

There was also a menace threatening France on the east. Russia, which up to now had been regarded by the more civilized countries as a land of barbarous tribes, had started to assert herself as a nation. Under Catherine the Great, these wild hordes had been brought into something like order, and now constituted a powerful foe. Catherine and Frederick were friends, and for France this was a formidable combination.

Something had to be done. Some readjustment among nations obviously must be considered. And it looked as if an alliance with Austria might be the solution. This was the point of view of the next king of France, Louis XV, and of some of his ministers.

In Austria the need for action was even greater. If Frederick was a questionable ally to France, he was a bitter enemy to Austria. To Maria Theresa, Frederick II was a monster. She never forgave him for taking away the Austrian province of Silesia. Without even declaring war he had walked in and taken it. He had seized Silesia as a dog seizes a bone. And maneuver as she would through the years, Maria Theresa was never able to get Silesia away from him. Wars were fought and won and lost. Treaties were made and signed and broken. But Frederick held Silesia in his teeth and he never let go.

Maria Theresa was therefore more than ready for an alliance with her old enemy France. Together they might defy Frederick. She admitted her desire openly. In France, however, opinion was divided. Austria had been an enemy too long, and the old anti-Austrian sentiment was still strong.

Nevertheless messages were sent back and forth between Vienna and Versailles, the French court. Couriers on horseback rode swiftly across Europe from east to west and back. Negotiations went on secretly for years. Finally in 1756 a treaty was signed: France and Austria were officially friends and allies.

At the time when this happened the baby who was one day to cement this friendship was not yet one year old.

From 1756 to 1770 Maria Theresa's great aim was to see a Hapsburg marry a Bourbon. In that day intermarriage in the royal families was the customary way of strengthening the bonds between countries. Kings or queens, emperors or empresses, ruled their countries with complete, unquestioned authority. Ministers might advise, and did. But the power lay strictly in the hands of the ruling family. It was the day of the absolute monarchy. As for the common people of all these countries, they took things as they came, because they had no choice. To place her daughter on the throne of France, Maria Theresa considered, would be her greatest political accomplishment. The dauphin was the oldest son and heir to the French throne. The title "dauphin" was like that of Prince of Wales in England. When Louis XV should die—and he was now sixty—the Dauphin would become the king of France, and Marie Antoinette, as his wife, would be the queen.

Marie Antoinette was on tiptoes with excitement over her approaching marriage. But she was not in the least frightened. That she was to be a queen when she grew up she had taken for granted, exactly as a girl nowadays takes for granted that after graduation she will find a job and later marry.

To be a queen was to Marie Antoinette her right and

her destiny. Three of her sisters had already married rulers. Caroline, her very closest companion, was now the Queen of Naples. (Both Joanna and Josepha, another sister, had been engaged in turn to marry the King of Naples, but both had died of smallpox.) Amalia was married to the Duke of Parma (also in Italy). And Christina was the wife of the Prince of Saxony. All of these marriages had been part and parcel of the political schemes of Maria Theresa in defiance of Frederick the Great. To provide for the *happiness* of her daughters had never entered her head.

To be the dauphiness of France and later queen of France naturally took preparation. During the last two years, when the politicians in both countries were reaching their goal, Marie Antoinette was being groomed for her future role. For the most part she lent herself gracefully to the task. But she did regret the loss of her beloved governess, Countess Brandeiss. In her place came a tutor, decided upon after many exchanges between the two courts. He was Abbé Vermond, a priest, who became Marie Antoinette's teacher, her confessor, her advisor and her friend, for this period before she married, and for many years afterwards.

He came to Vienna at Christmastime from the south of France, a kindly man, dark-skinned and dark-haired, and clumsy in his long priestly robe. The city lay under a covering of snow when he arrived, and the jingle of sleighbells and the clinking of horses' hoofs on hard ice filled the air. He stood on the balcony of the Hofburg beside the Empress looking down on the snow-covered streets. Maria Theresa was a large hearty woman who did not feel the cold, but the thinly clad priest from warmer climes was shivering. Together they were watching the approach of a sleigh drawn by two spanking horses and driven by a coachman in livery with a footman beside him. In the sleigh, a fur robe pulled up to her chin, her cheeks red with cold and health, was the Abbé's little pupil-to-be. Marie Antoinette pulled out her hand and waved it gaily, and even from that distance the two at once became friends.

Abbé Vermond's first duty was to hear her confession. But what sins could a little girl of thirteen have committed? He was touched by her innocence and her beauty.

"She has a most graceful figure," he wrote back to France. "She holds herself well; and if (as may be hoped) she grows a little taller, she will have all the good qualities one could wish for in a great princess!"

As she was still growing, Abbé Vermond measured her height from time to time and sent the results back to his own country.

But charming as Marie Antoinette was, she gave the Abbé considerable trouble. She still managed as before to slip out of school work. The Abbé was there to teach her French, French history, and the ways of the French court. But one hour of work a day was all he could hold her down to. She was docile, seemingly willing, and happy to be with the soft-spoken Abbé. But she could not keep her mind on study. The habit of industry had never been taught her.

"She is more intelligent than has been generally supposed," he wrote back to France, adding with certain restraint: "Unfortunately up to the age of twelve she has not been trained to concentrate in any way. Since she is rather lazy and frivolous she is hard to teach . . . I cannot induce her to take the trouble to get to the bottom of a subject on her own initiative, though I feel that it is well within her power to do so. I have come to recognize that she will only learn so long as she is being amused."

She eventually learned to speak French well. "Only a few awkward expressions remain," wrote back the Abbé. "These she will give up when she no longer hears the German and the bad French of those around her."

But her handwriting! "She writes inconceivably slow," he reported.

Poor little Marie Antoinette! Her handwriting became notorious. To this day samples of it can still be seen. Big unformed childish letters—even after she was grown up!

But for a French court, looks and deportment were of far more importance than learning. Marie Antoinette's teeth had to be straightened by a French dentist. This took three months. Her waist had to be laced in because she was no longer to be a tomboy running, but a lady bowing. A hairdresser was imported from Paris, which marks the beginning of an outstanding interest in hair arrangements. She was drilled in curtsies and in court etiquette.

At some of this training our young archduchess was particularly apt. She had a good memory and much grace of personality. The pleasant answer came easily.

"Over which country would you prefer to be queen?" her mother asked her as a test.

"I would choose France because it is the country of Henry IV and Louis XIV—the one so great, the other so good!" It had almost a copybook exactness.

Then there was the matter of her dowry, her trousseau, her jewels. As we shall see, jewels were of vast importance in royal circles. But at this point Marie Antoinette was not interested in adornment, though her taste for it grew with the years.

All in all she was having—up to the 19th of April, the day she was officially married—just the kind of fun any young girl has when she becomes engaged, especially when she is the darling of the gods, as Marie Antoinette seemed to be—parties, clothes, attention. She had no inhibitions, no self-consciousness, no embarrassment. She loved everybody and was in turn beloved.

During the last week before her marriage she slept every night with her mother. Probably in those few nights the two were closer than ever before in their lives. Maria Theresa was no doubt counseling her, making up for the neglect of fourteen years. But no one knows.

Then came the wedding day at the Church of the

Augustines. The Dauphin himself was not present at his own marriage. It was a marriage by proxy, as was common custom in those days. The Archduke Ferdinand, as we saw, knelt in his place and received for him the blessing of the Pope.

Two days later came her departure. The big cavalcade that was to start her on her way from Vienna to Versailles had been assembled and was now about to get under way. The streets of the city were strewn with flowers and lined with people. But strangely enough the people were sad.

"The capital of Austria looks like a city in mourning," said someone who was there that day. Once more a shadow passed across the sun. The people were downcast instead of merry. There were premonitions.

This was April 21st. At half-past nine in the morning the little girl said goodbye to her mother and her city. Neither of them was she ever to see again.

In her pocket was a note from her mother which she read as the carriage moved away. "Farewell, dearest child," it said. "You will be far, far away. Be just, be kind, never forget the obligations of your royal rank . . . be so good to the French people that they will say I have sent them an angel. . . ."

When the last fine carriage had passed beyond the limits of Vienna, Maria Theresa went alone to church. Was it to thank God for the success of her plans? Or was it to beg forgiveness for her neglect?

Probably it was to pray that God might avert disaster

from this, her youngest child. For a second letter caught up with Marie Antoinette before she reached her destination. "My daughter, in the time of misfortune think of me!"

her new costume, and now they kissed the hand of their young mistress for the last time and backed away into their anteroom.

It was only then that the little girl lost her poise. As the last familiar face disappeared she burst into tears and threw herself onto the breast of the Countess Noailles, much to the consternation of that dignified lady.

It was natural enough that a young girl should throw herself into the arms of the one person who now represented a tie with the past—the one into whose care her mother had entrusted her. But Marie Antoinette was to be a queen and she knew her responsibilities. Summoning all her will power, she swallowed her despair. "Pardon me," she cried, trying to smile through her tears. "These are for the family and the fatherland I am leaving. For the future I shall not forget that I am French!"

Everyone Austrian had now left her. The French took over. And she entered the country a Frenchwoman, destined never again to leave France.

In France the cavalcade was even more splendid than in Austria, and in all the towns the people gathered to watch it pass. King Louis XV had sent two magnificent coaches to bring his young granddaughter-in-law-to-be and her coterie from the Rhine to Versailles. Rare wood, gilded springs, painted linings—nothing was left undone to assure this maiden that it was royal France that was greeting her. Through the high windows of the first coach the people saw her smiling face, her forehead of matchless purity, her bright cheeks, her bluest of blue eyes. Children threw flowers before her, young girls came out to dance, the crowds cheered in joy.

The roads over which she traveled were main roads, well kept. To venture on to side roads would have been difficult traveling, for these were narrow and muddy and rutted. It would also have been a mistake to look too closely at some of the peasants whom they passed. Such poverty, if she had really understood it, would have been too terrible a contrast. But the beautiful carriages rolled smoothly along, and the crowds continued to cheer.

Marie Antoinette looked out on the broad green fields of the countryside that was now her land, and at the new faces in the towns. She was happy again and on the alert. She never failed to say the right word.

In one of the first cities the mayor addressed her formally in German. "Do not speak German, Monsieur," she said, smiling. "From today I understand no other language but French."

They passed through Reims. Reims was the coronation city, where her husband would be crowned king, and she, queen, when the present king should die. "This town," she said tactfully, "is the one of all France which I hope not to see again for the longest possible time!"

She meant so well! She was so willing to meet them all more than halfway!

When the Austrian ambassador, Count Mercy, heard the glowing accounts of the journey from members of the party, he quickly sent a report to Maria Theresa. "Our archduchess-dauphiness has surpassed all our hopes!" he wrote. (Of Count Mercy and his many letters to Maria Theresa we shall hear more and more as time goes on.)

At Compiègne the greatest ordeal of all awaited her. Here was the royal family waiting. Here were the Bourbons, proud rulers of France. Here was King Louis XV, now her monarch, and the Dauphin, her husband. And once again the young girl carried it off victoriously.

The meeting took place in the forest, and when Marie Antoinette saw the King's carriage, she jumped out of her own, ran lightly over to his, and bowed low before him. It was her own instinctive reaction—an unrehearsed act of grace—and as such it delighted the old King.

He was truly charmed. To Louis XV, coming from the court of Versailles where women's beauty was heavily artificial, this slender girl with bright unrouged cheeks and pale blonde hair must have been like a breath from the Austrian spring—of apple-blossoms and of violets deep in meadow grass.

The King raised her to her feet, embraced her and

Marie Antoinette bowed low before the King

presented her to the Dauphin, her husband, who in turn also kissed her—but awkwardly and unwillingly.

It was a boy just sixteen whom Marie Antoinette saw on that first momentous day. He was big like most of the Bourbons, and heavy-set. He didn't stand erect and when he walked his head was thrust forward. He was near-sighted and his eyes were watery and heavy-lidded. His hair was untidy. It was always untidy in spite of royal hairdressers, as Marie Antoinette was to learn in the days ahead. But by far his greatest handicap was that he knew he was gawky, which made him more so. Unlike his child-bride, he could not meet people easily. He knew nothing of the ways of the world.

Of course Marie Antoinette could not know these inner workings of the boy before her, nor could she know what lay back of his extreme timidity and lack of self-confidence. But to those who knew the circumstances of his life, the cause was obvious.

Louis, the Dauphin, had been brought up in isolation. His parents had disapproved of the frivolous life of the Louis XV Versailles court, and so lived in the country in retirement, taking care of their children's education themselves. They both died before Louis was thirteen, and the tutor in whose charge the children were left continued faithfully in the same way—that is, to bring up the boy apart from the world and people.

There could be no greater handicap for a ruler.

Louis had none of the attributes of a king. For all his big size he had little energy. He suffered from inertia which affected both his physical motions and his ability to make decisions. A gland specialist today might have known how to correct his troubles. A psychiatrist would have been able to help him. But when he kissed Marie Antoinette in the forest of Compiègne, he was far from Prince Charming. He was just an uncouth boy who suddenly found himself married to the most beautiful young girl in European royal circles.

Versailles, their destination, was a two days' journey from Compiègne. Marie Antoinette sat in the front seat of the great coach between grandfather and grandson, between King Louis XV and the future King Louis XVI. In the old man's hat flashed the Pitt diamond, the most famous jewel in the world at that time. But it was no brighter than his eye as he chatted with his pretty young companion. The Dauphin stared ahead, tongue-tied and uneasy.

It was not an intimate home-coming. Versailles is probably the largest palace in Europe. It still stands, twelve miles from Paris, for all to see the vanity and the magnificence of kings. It is a mighty mass of buildings —galleries, wings, halls, courts, apartments, huge rooms, high ceilings, great arches—surrounded by a magnificent garden of trees, lawns, shrubbery, statues, fountains, paths. When Marie Antoinette came to it, 5,000 people lived in the palace, the stables housed 2,000 horses, and 3,000 to 4,000 servants stood passive in gorgeous livery.

Versailles was gargantuan. Size of course gives a palace a certain magnificence. But aside from its rooms of state it was not beautiful. It was not comfortable. From what people who lived and visited there have written—and how those eighteenth century people wrote!—we know that all the living apartments except those of the royal family itself were dark and dirty, hot in summer, cold in winter; the walls were thin and every whisper could be heard; the air was bad; what plumbing there was was poor and the smells evil.

This was not only the home of the king and his family and his relations, but of all his courtiers and their families and their servants, as well as of would-be courtiers who gave up good homes of their own in distant parts of France and came here to try their luck at court. Its doors were open to the world. Along the stairways and in the passages tradespeople sold their wares, as in a bazaar. Crowds wandered at large through the great halls and corridors, rich, poor, well-dressed courtiers and shabby townsfolk. This was permitted, not in a spirit of democratic friendliness, but as a gesture of royal beneficence: let the people enter as they enter a church! Let them see their king!

This pretentious monstrosity of a dwelling was to be young Marie Antoinette's home supposedly for the rest of her life. It was about as cozy as living in the Pentagon, about as private as a railroad terminal.

The entire family was present when she arrived. These were only cardboard figures to her then—those who later were to take on personalities of vital importance. There were the three aunts of her husband—the three middle-aged spinster daughters of King Louis, known to all as Mesdames. There were the Dauphin's two younger brothers, the Count of Provence and the Count of Artois, boys of fourteen and thirteen; and his two little sisters, Clothilde and Elisabeth, both still in their governess's care. Present also were cousins—dukes and duchesses, princes and princesses, counts and countesses, of Orléans, Condé, Conti, Chartres, La Marche, Penthièvre, Lamballe—names that were famous in France's history, people of power and distinction who within the next twenty-five years would face extinction. What Marie Antoinette saw as she entered Versailles was the last page of royal history which within her own short span would come to its bitter end.

Within a few hours of her arrival Marie Antoinette was married for the second time, this time in the Chapel of Louis XIV in the palace, with the real Dauphin kneeling beside her. It was May 16, 1770. The Archbishop of Reims blessed the young couple and said Mass, the royal choir sang, and attendant bishops held a canopy of silver brocade above their heads. Only the highest nobles were present, though the crowd could be heard pressing and murmuring outside the chapel door.

When the marriage was over the King signed the marriage contract and the blood relatives in order of precedence signed their names below his. Beside the big unformed letters that read "Marie Antoinette Josepha Jeanne" was a big blot of ink. Poor Marie Antoinette and her handwriting! The parchment contract still exists and the blot, in our later knowledge, looks ominous.

Bad luck attended the ceremonies that surrounded the marriage. Great crowds had poured out twelve miles from Paris to Versailles to see the festivities. Paris itself was deserted. Shops were closed. This was a gala day. But a violent storm burst in the afternoon, the worst storm Versailles had ever known. Thunder roared and the rain fell in torrents. The crowds ran for shelter, pushing and shouting. No fireworks could be set off and the rain put out all the illuminations.

Indoors, however, all was under control. Eager courtiers filled the long mirrored rooms; thousands of candles lighted their jewels; a magnificent supper was served. Only twenty-two actually sat down to eat—members of the royal family—while 6,000 nobles reverently watched.

Two weeks after the marriage ceremony a disaster far greater than a thunderstorm befell the Parisians. Since they had lost out on the festivities at Versailles, it was planned that the city of Paris should have its own celebration. It was to be staged in the Place Louis XV in the center of which rose a large seated figure of the King. (This was later called Place de la Révolution, and is now Place de la Concorde. It is probably the most famous, certainly one of the most beautiful squares in the world.)

Paris at that time had a population of 600,000 and as

many of that number as could had planned to come to the celebration. A large crowd had already gathered in the afternoon, with more and more people continuing to pour in as darkness fell.

Elaborate fireworks were to be set off in front of the statue of Louis in the center of the square. In the meantime they had been stored in a wooden building put up for that purpose behind the statue. This now contained set-pieces, fountains of fire, Roman candles, enormous pinwheels. But everything went wrong. One large bouquet went off ahead of time, and nothing followed. None of the principal set-pieces would light.

Some of the crowd, impatient from standing so long, now tried to get out and go home while others, still coming, pushed their way in. There was only one outlet to the square and that was torn up while a street was being paved. Huge piles of stone and sand cluttered it and the open ditches dug for sewerage. As the incoming and outgoing crowds met, it was impossible to move in any direction.

It was at this point that the building which held the reserves of fireworks caught fire. The flames blazed high and a spectacle of unpremeditated brilliance lighted the square. Fire engines clanging their bells charged into the crowd and behind them carriages with drivers seeking their masters in the mob. People were trampled upon, thrown into the ditches; children screamed for their lost parents and horses neighed in fright.

All night long the stampede continued. Hundreds of

wounded were taken to hospitals, and when the square was finally emptied, one hundred and thirty-two corpses lay on the stone pavements. It was morning. The corpses were buried in the cemetery of the Madeleine Church.

Marie Antoinette had been looking forward eagerly to the Paris fireworks. With the three aunts she had driven in from Versailles and as they approached the city and saw the red sky, she urged the coachman to drive faster, thinking the celebration had already started. Not until they reached the Seine did they hear of the catastrophe. There they saw people running through the streets crying. The sound of distant screaming came to their ears like wails from an inferno.

The horses' heads were turned back. It was the first time Marie Antoinette had entered Paris. Three years would pass before she would enter it again.

4

The Lonely Years

Versailles was a golden cage. The door was kept closed so that the bird could not escape. But eyes from without stared and kept watch.

It was four o'clock in the afternoon and Abbé Vermond in his long black soutane had just entered Marie Antoinette's sitting room. Though Dauphiness of France, she still had to have her lessons.

The girl was standing at the window that looked out on the paved court now shining with rain. Her eyes were overbright.

When the Abbé put a kindly hand on her shoulder, her tension was released. She ran to the sofa and burst into tears.

"My mother has scolded me again!" she sobbed. "She is too hard!"

With her wet handkerchief clutched in her hand she reached for the letters she had rumpled from much reading and handed them to the Abbé. "She makes me sound like an animal!"

The Abbé looked down the page. "Try to furnish your mind with a little good reading," he read in Maria Theresa's by now familiar bold script. "It is more necessary for you than others since you do not know music, or drawing, or dancing, or painting, or any pleasing accomplishment . . . You must ask the Abbé to send me an account every month of what you have finished and of what you intend to begin."

"How does she know I haven't read them!" Marie Antoinette sobbed.

They both looked at the pile of books that lay on her desk. They were just as the Abbé had left them the day before—untouched. "How does she *know?*"

The Abbé shook his head and turned back to the letters. ". . . the handwriting of your letters becomes every day worse and less correct. In these ten months you should have improved. You must practice with the Abbé to form a better hand, and to write more evenly."

Again he shook his head. All her childhood this girl had never been taught to write properly, nor had a love of books ever been encouraged. How in ten months could she change, as her mother demanded! As Dauphiness of France she must command the respect of a famous court, but as her mother's daughter she must do as she was told! "What will people think!" she cried.

Only when she had calmed down could they start the lessons. Much of their hour together was already gone.

Life at Versailles—even among 5,000 persons—was lonely for the little Dauphiness. But she was too proud to complain. Always so happy with her sisters at Schönbrunn, she now found herself among strangers, almost alone, with no other girl her own age to talk to.

She wrote to Caroline in Naples. But Caroline was a queen involved in her own disturbing affairs, and had no time for a young sister. She wrote to her beloved Brandeiss who answered with long comforting letters. Then suddenly the Brandeiss letters stopped coming. Marie Antoinette waited, looked in vain in the mail from Vienna, wrote again and again, and finally despaired. Everyone had deserted her!

But not everyone! Not everyone had forgotten the little Dauphiness, now the blood tie between the great kingdoms of Austria and France! From distant Vienna Maria Theresa was keeping closer watch on her daughter than she ever had when the child was under the same roof. Maria Theresa knew everything that went on at Versailles. She knew what Marie Antoinette read and did not read, what dresses she wore, what conversations she had and with whom, what she ate, and how she and the Dauphin, and she and the aunts, and she and the King, were getting along. Up to the day of her death Maria Theresa was in constant touch. If she had read Marie Antoinette's most intimate diary, if she had been in an alcove listening, she could not have known more than she did.

And how was this accomplished?

It was an elaborate system of espionage that this mother was playing on her daughter. Her chief in command was Count Mercy, ambassador from Austria to Versailles, a bachelor with no wife to interfere, an able, intelligent man devoted to Maria Theresa, his employer and his Empress. He was friendly with the young Dauphiness who liked him as a nice old man and the friend of her mother. He was her advisor, one step above Abbé Vermond who was merely teacher and confessor. It was Mercy's duty not only to report all manner of details to Vienna, but also to advise Marie Antoinette. When he found his advice was making no impression, he appealed to Maria Theresa, who would at once take the matter in hand and write a letter to her daughter, never mentioning Count Mercy.

"It is most fortunate," he wrote, "that Madame the Dauphiness honors us with her confidence."

Not only did Marie Antoinette talk to him freely. He also had many other avenues of information. "I have made sure of three persons in the service of the Archduchess," he wrote the Empress soon after life in Versailles had settled into a routine. "One of her women and two of her men-servants, who give me full reports of what goes on. Then from day to day I am told of the conversations she has with Abbé Vermond, from whom she hides nothing. Besides this the Marquise of Durfort passes on to me everything she says to her aunts. I have also sources of information as to what goes on whenever the Dauphiness sees the King. Superadded are my personal observations, so that there really is not an hour of the day as to which I am not instructed concerning what the Archduchess may have said or done or heard . . ."

Because mail was sometimes opened in its long journey across Europe, Count Mercy and the Empress used secret messengers. Even the Emperor Joseph knew nothing of their correspondence. And poor little Marie Antoinette, properly fearful of her powerful mother, never knew how she came to know so much about her and such intimate details. Of all people she would never have suspected Count Mercy because her mother had said unequivocally that he told her nothing. And how could a daughter fail to believe the word of her own mother?

But it was upsetting. Marie Antoinette knew that someone was spying on her and she lived in perpetual distrust of those around her.

The letters from Countess Brandeiss stopped because Maria Theresa forbade the Austrian governess ever again to write to her old pupil. But of course Marie Antoinette never knew.

Count Mercy felt sorry for the girl. "She feels she is not much loved," he wrote tentatively to his Empress. "She feels she will always be treated with severity."

At one point Kaunitz, the Austrian Prime Minister, advised Maria Theresa to stop scolding her daughter. He was an old man now and not afraid even of his Empress. "It is quite useless," he told her. "It will only make her angry."

"My heart aches for her," wrote Abbé Vermond.

But Maria Theresa persisted. To the bitter end she continued to exhort, to badger, to scold the girl she had failed to bring up properly.

In place of Countess Brandeiss, Marie Antoinette now had her Countess Noailles, the staid, dignified, worthy noblewoman who had met her at the Rhine River. No one in Versailles was better equipped to tell a young dauphiness how to act, how to dress, how to speak, what to say and to whom to say it. But her earnestness in trying to make over her young charge was too much for a normal girl like Marie Antoinette.

Marie Antoinette was by no means always in tears. She was by nature too gay for that. Her troubles were soon forgotten and her need for fun almost always won out. This frivolity, in turn, was too much for Countess Noailles.

It was only a short time back that Marie Antoinette was little Antoine running with the dogs at Schönbrunn. Now Countess Noailles was shocked when the girl walked in the park of Versailles with only one companion. When one day she lost a shoe while chasing a butterfly, the countess was so flustered that she went to the King with her problem.

"Sire," she began. "A princess called upon to ascend the throne has to fulfill duties which will make her revered before she reaches the supreme rank!"

The old King knew where this obscure talk was leading. "And what duties, Countess, do you mean to impose on a woman a little over fifteen?" he asked good-naturedly. "Let her dance! Let her surround herself with gentle madcaps!"

Let her dance . . . A girl of fifteen needed exercise. She needed fresh air. Marie Antoinette loved to ride and she rode well, but at Versailles she was refused permission. From far-off Vienna her mother wrote Mercy *not* to let her daughter endanger her life by riding. Mercy told the Foreign Minister, and the Foreign Minister told the King. "We'll let her ride a donkey then!" the King conceded. So the little horsewoman ignominiously mounted a small gray donkey.

One day she whipped her donkey into such a run that he objected and threw her.

As she picked herself up she laughed. "Go call Countess Noailles," she called out to her ladies. "Ask her what is the etiquette when a Dauphiness of France falls off a donkey!"

But no one else laughed. No one was willing to play with her. Whenever she tried to make a joke someone pulled a long face. She called Countess Noailles "Madame Etiquette." But no one was amused. A sense of humor is a dangerous mark in the rarefied circles of royalty.

Let her surround herself with gentle madcaps . . . But there were no madcaps—yet.

Marie Antoinette's closest companions during the first two years of her new French life were the three aunts of the Dauphin, the three middle-aged spinster daughters of the King. They were Madame Adelaide, Madame Victoire, and Madame Sophie. Horace Walpole, the visiting Englishman, called them "clumsy plump old wenches, awkward, confused, not knowing what to do or say." The King, being their father, allowed them a few minutes of his time each day, but the rest of the court neglected them entirely. In retaliation they gossiped and plotted. They schemed. They annoyed others with small insect-like biting. The time was to come when their evil spirits would nurture tragedy. But at this point they were more mosquitoes than tarantulas.

Madame Adelaide was the dominant one of the three.

The King's spinster daughters were her bad fairies

She craved power and had none. Her frustration consequently made her dangerous. As she disliked all Austrians, she now sought the deadliest way of destroying the one Austrian who had come into her web.

Madame Victoire was big and fat. She liked her food and her armchair. She was too lazy to do anything but follow the lead of Adelaide.

Sophie was timid, morose, silent. Whether or not she agreed with Adelaide was of no consequence because she herself was of complete unimportance.

These were the companions of pretty young Marie Antoinette. These were her three bad fairies. Because they had lived so long by themselves in seclusion, they had learned to hide their feelings, so she had no inkling of their strong dislike. In fact their first gesture in her direction was destined to make them her friends. They gave her a key to their apartments in the palace so that she might come to them in privacy without her ladies-in-waiting. This gave them an unparalleled opportunity to discover her every weakness, and at the same time pleased Marie Antoinette. To have someone want her was all that she could ask for in those days. She spent most of her leisure with them and was as frank and spontaneous with them as with her own family. In her innocence she would make fun of certain courtiers and go into paroxysms of laughter. Because she needed to laugh she made her own jokes. Such high spirits got on Adelaide's nerves, but none the less she encouraged the girl to chatter. Impulsive, free of calculation, Marie

Antoinette thus laid herself open to mischief-makers, to gossipers, eventually to scandalmongers.

For lack of other madcaps the Dauphiness played with her "mops." Mops were the fashionable dogs of the day—lap dogs with snub noses, like small pugs. As controlled in their actions as their mistress was, they were allowed to play only in her apartment, nowhere else. But that section of the greatest palace in the world they made their own. They dug into the rugs, tore holes in the tapestry and damask covering, scratched the carved and gilded legs of chairs, covered the parquet floors with paw marks, ripped Marie Antoinette's dresses. They were her constant delight. She loved them so much that she asked Count Mercy to get her two more from Austria.

"There's *some* way of getting them here, isn't there?" she pleaded, when she saw the Count's frigid reaction.

"I informed Her Royal Highness," he wrote to Maria Theresa, "that the channel of the passengers unquestionably furnished a means." Poor Mercy! He not only had to make a queen out of this wisp of a girl. He must now undertake dogs!

Dresses were almost as much a burden as manners. In Vienna the Hapsburgs dressed up only for visitors or for formal occasions. At Versailles everyone was formal twenty-four hours a day, with costumes that were monumental in their importance. "Let me at least have my *un*dress private costumes in the morning," Marie Antoinette begged the King.

At court she was obliged to wear royal robes heavy with jewels and stiff with stays. But the minute she got back in her own rooms after a court function she threw them off. "Thank heavens, I am out of harness!" she would cry, to Countess Noailles' horror.

Whalebone, for stays, was bought for the ladies of the court by the carload. Some of them may have needed it to pull in their too well-fed figures. But not Marie Antoinette who was slender as a reed, and as graceful. However, her mother heard about her objections, and immediately sent a letter commanding her to wear stays lest her figure be spoiled!

The Hapsburgs dressed simply and they ate frugally. But not the Bourbons who were greedy and nearly all overweight. They ate slowly and abundantly. They drank wine steadily through a meal. Beside them Marie Antoinette was as abstemious as a nun. She drank no wine. Her breakfast was just coffee or chocolate with little biscuits to dip in; dinner was the same; and for supper she took a plate of soup with the white meat of chicken.

Not all the Bourbons, however, were yet obese. Not all of them were old. The Dauphin's two brothers were younger and gayer than the Dauphin, particularly the Count of Artois, and often played with their young sister-in-law as was natural for their age.

Beside his brothers and this fun-loving girl, the Dauphin was a clout. Actually he was a nice boy, and his awkward appearance did him an injustice. He was good. He had a deep sense of justice. His instincts were right. Like Marie Antoinette he had a good mind, and unlike her he had been taught how to use it. He knew Latin thoroughly, he understood Italian and could speak German. His English was so good that he later translated several English books. But he was too shy to look people in the eye. Because he was near-sighted he would have had to look too closely, so instead he shifted his glance away. This gave him an appearance of craftiness which was farthest possible from his real nature. He was terrified of the King, his grandfather; and the ministers, courtiers and ambassadors paralyzed him. He was ill at ease with his wife and had nothing to say to her.

Whether or not some of this indifference was due to his aunts we have no way of knowing. He had always been very much under their influence and they were, as we do know, the underground leaders opposed to "the Austrian."

His diary remains, which from time to time in face of the great events of his life gives us a glimpse into his curious backwardness.

On the first day that he saw Marie Antoinette all he wrote was: "Interview with Madame the Dauphine."

On the morning after their first night at Versailles he said to her: "Have you slept?"

"Yes," she answered.

Having no more to say he left her, and Marie Antoinette, uncomfortable and unhappy, began to play with her dog. (This conversation was one of the many that Count Mercy wrote word for word to her mother.)

Marie Antoinette was hurt at her husband's lack of interest in her. They were both lonely but they could not yet find each other. Maria Theresa was upset, not because the young couple might be unhappy, but because relationship between the two countries might suffer thereby.

Marie Antoinette had been living three years in Versailles before she was allowed to go to Paris. She was only twelve miles away—one hour by carriage. But the aunts insisted on her remaining at court, and persuaded their father not to give his permission for her to leave. They feared her popularity with the crowds, who always idolize youth and beauty. If she should go to Paris they feared for their own small power.

And how right they were! When Marie Antoinette did finally get to Paris her triumph soared above her highest hopes.

It was May, 1773, when Marie Antoinette took matters in her own hand. She was now seventeen, and three years married. To see Paris had become an obsession with her ever since she had come to France and now she refused to be put off any longer. Her method was direct. She did not appeal to the aunts whom she was now beginning to suspect. Instead she went straight to the King and asked him if she could possibly go to Paris.

It seemed little enough to ask. If she had done it a year before it would have worked as well. The King considered her request only reasonable. He gave his permission and left it to her to make the plans.

The date was set for June 8th, but her excitement was so keen that she couldn't wait. She had the King's permission, why not take advantage of it?

With some difficulty she persuaded the Dauphin, and with no difficulty whatsoever she persuaded his younger brother, the Count of Artois, to take her on a secret visit. From her hairdresser she had heard about "opera balls"—balls in Paris where the people wore masks and no one knew who anyone else was. So the three royal youngsters ordered a carriage for late at night, dressed up in play costumes which Marie Antoinette got together for them, and drove to Paris. There they went to an "opera ball."

The next morning the three appeared at Mass, their eyes demurely down, and no one in authority knew of their breathless escapade.

The legitimate trip to Paris was all that a princess could have dreamed. The news spread that the Dauphin and Dauphiness were coming and all the way from Versailles to Paris crowds lined the way, throwing their hats jubilantly in the air, shouting with pleasure. It was a beautiful sunny day, and the reflection of sun and happiness on the face of the young girl was ravishing. In Paris they went directly to the Tuileries, the city palace of the Bourbons, and because of the shouts outside the young couple stepped out on the balcony to wave their hands to the crowd awaiting them.

The thousands of upturned faces were almost frightening. "*Mon Dieu*, how many of them there are!" the Dauphiness cried.

An old general stood beside her. "Madame," he said gallantly, "you have before you two hundred thousand persons who have all fallen in love with you!"

This was her first inkling of what it might mean to be the queen of France.

"Last Tuesday," she wrote her mother, "there was a festival which I shall never forget. We made our entry into Paris . . . Dear mother, I do not know how to describe to you the delight and affection! . . . Such love is infinitely precious . . . I shall never forget it!"

This was a turning point. As far as Marie Antoinette's docility was concerned, this was the beginning of the end.

5

The Butterfly Queen

"The king is dead! Long live the king!"

The Dauphin sat with Marie Antoinette in their own apartment at Versailles awaiting word. For thirteen days the old king had been ill of smallpox, that deadly menace that Marie Antoinette knew so tragically from her own childhood days.

The King had not permitted them to come into his room because of the infection. Only the three aunts, his daughters, remained with their father (and caught the disease from him, though they did not die).

So now the young couple sat together waiting. They seldom were alone. They saw very little of each other in this strange royal marriage of theirs. But now, waiting, they looked at each other shyly. The grimness of age and death drew them together, and the drama of what lay ahead.

Smallpox polluted the air. Fifty persons in the palace had come down with it, and ten of them died. But the danger, great as it was, did not prevent the courtiers from flocking to Versailles. Now they crowded into the antechamber of the dying King. It was not affection that brought them but curiosity and self-interest. If and when there was to be a turn in the affairs of court the courtiers wanted to be on the spot. The room into which they were packed was called the Oeil de Boeuf, the eye of the bull, because of its oval window. It was outside the King's own chamber and here it was that the news and gossip of the court were exchanged. It was here that they now waited impatiently.

Suddenly the Dauphin and Marie Antoinette were startled by what began as a rumble and became a thunderous roar. It was the courtiers rushing out from the Oeil de Boeuf and through the corridors of the palace. The King's death had finally been announced.

From hundreds of lips came the cry, "The king is dead! Long live the king!"

Uncertainly the young couple stood up facing the door, Marie Antoinette with her hands clasped to her bosom, Louis solid and heavy and flushed.

Then the door burst open and Countess Noailles ran in breathlessly. She threw herself at the feet of the Dauphin, now become her king.

The blackened corpse of Louis XV was quickly removed from the palace. There was no ceremony. He was gone and no one was sorry except the three sick daughters.

Because of the swift spread of infection in Versailles the royal family moved at once to La Muette, a palace in the Bois de Boulogne close to Paris. Day after day large crowds trudged out from the city to see their new monarchs and to cheer them. The people of France looked to these young rulers to wave a magic wand. Louis XV had been a dissolute monarch and his reign of nearly sixty years disastrous for the welfare of the country. The prestige of France abroad, which had soared during the reign of Louis XIV, went steadily down during the reign of his successor. Louis XIV had been a strong ruler and a resolute man. He had waged successful wars, sent colonists out into the new world, and for a time brought France prosperity and wealth. Now the country's finances were in a dangerous state and the load of taxation was more than the people could carry.

All eyes turned toward the new King and Queen. The people knew that the King was a good man, simple in his tastes and kind, and they were proud to have such a beautiful queen. Even the most pessimistic were hopeful. Things couldn't be worse, they said to one another. They must be better. And the cheering continued.

Marie Antoinette was deeply impressed. "To think," she wrote her mother, "that I, the least of your children, have been chosen to be queen over the finest realm in Europe!"

But Maria Theresa from her distance saw the situation more clearly than either the people of France or their queen. She could also be depended upon to take down her daughter. "I do *not* compliment you on your new dignity," she wrote back. "You are both of you still extremely young and the burden is a heavy one. I am distressed, much distressed . . . All I can say is: change nothing, let matters go on as they are. Otherwise you will find yourselves in such a tangle that you will be unable to extricate yourselves."

It was indeed a heavy burden—an enormous responsibility—for a king of twenty who had always lived apart from the world, and was by nature irresolute; and a queen of nineteen who had no inclination whatsoever for politics.

The Butterfly Queen

The actual crowning of Louis XVI took place in May, 1775, according to custom nearly a year after the old king's death. He was crowned in the coronation city of Reims, the city which Marie Antoinette had entered as a bride on her way to Versailles, and where she had been so tactful. "I hope that this will be the *last* city of France that I will visit!" Here she was, four years later, as France's queen.

Athough she was queen Marie Antoinette was not crowned beside her husband. She was glad to be an onlooker. Nevertheless it was she, the tall fair-haired beautiful queen, more than Louis, the heavy-footed king, whom the crowd cheered and followed through the streets of Reims.

"I shall never forget the day of the coronation during my whole life if it should last two hundred years!" Marie Antoinette wrote her mother.

But again Maria Theresa was not cheering. "The situation of the king, of the ministers and even of the State, exhibits nothing that is reassuring," she wrote to Mercy. "I fear her happy days are over."

But her happy days, as Marie Antoinette saw them then, were just beginning. Happiness to her meant freedom. For the first time in her life she could do as she pleased. No one could say her nay. She had a husband who was proud of her at last. She ruled a court of thousands—a court of richly dressed, frivolous, witty courtiers. She was Queen of France!

That she was at the head of a great nation of which she did not understand a single problem did not trouble her. The serious responsibilities of her position she did not see. She was gay and light-hearted and eager with anticipated delights.

Louis on the other hand did have a certain comprehension of the situation which the country and its monarchs were facing. He spent three or four hours every morning going over state papers. He had a grasp of the financial difficulties. But he did not have the strength of character to back up his ideas. He might see a solution for a knotty problem, but if a minister or a bishop or (more likely) an aunt argued against it, he let himself be swayed and often made a decision exactly contrary to his own better judgment. He was a good man and one of the most honest kings that ever sat on a throne. But he was sadly unsure.

Marie Antoinette's first move as a queen was to slide out from under the weight of court etiquette. It was a natural step for a normal woman. But is a queen a normal woman? And may she act naturally? In the eighteenth century these were important questions.

Up to now every detail of a French queen's life had been prescribed by rule. Every dress she wore, every chair she sat in, was prearranged. Every servant had a spot to stand in and a single duty to perform. Each lady-in-waiting knew her place, and only the highest ranking lady present could hand the queen so much as her handkerchief.

The queen's day, according to our modern standards, was preposterous. For one thing she had no privacy. When she awoke in the morning, usually about eight o'clock, a woman of the wardrobe entered with a basket containing underwear. Then came another with a book in which were pasted samples of dresses. For each season there were twelve full dress costumes; twelve "undress" dresses; twelve evening dresses. The queen now marked the three she chose for the day. Next a tub was rolled in. This was called the "sabot" because it was shaped like a shoe. Behind it came the women who were to bathe her, for this was the ceremony of the bath.

At nine o'clock she breakfasted, with six or seven persons standing around her watching.

The climax of the morning was the *lever*—the grand toilet. Folded chairs were brought in for this. They were placed in a circle about the queen, and in them sat the ladies-of-honor and of the bed-chamber, the princes, the captains of the guard, and all the visiting officials from other countries who had come to pay court. Thus surrounded Marie Antoinette had her hair done, quite an undertaking in itself; and after that, at the hands of the ladies-of-honor, she was dressed.

She then went to Mass. Still accompanied by the ladies-of-honor and of the bed-chamber, the ladies-of-the-palace, her gentlemen-in-waiting, her chief equerry, her own special clergy and the princesses of the royal family, the Queen walked down the corridors of the palace, through the long mirrored salon, to the chapel. Her prayers were her own.

After Mass came dinner, which to Marie Antoinette, who disliked to eat anyway, was the greatest horror of all. She and the King, every day, had to eat in public. Any "decently dressed" persons who wanted to could enter the dining room. It was one of the great sights for out-of-town visitors, like going up the Empire State Tower in New York or visiting Niagara Falls. After watching the King and Queen eat their soup, the visitors usually went rushing through the halls of the palace to the apartments of the King's brothers and their wives to see them eat their next course, and from there tore on to Mesdames, the aunts, to see them wolf down their dessert. Fortunately the Bourbons all liked to eat, so the sightseers got something for their pains. But for Marie Antoinette, who only picked at her food, it was torture.

Here she was, a young woman full of fun, ready to laugh, treated like a creature in the zoo!

Her first break with etiquette was to omit the public dressing. As soon as her hair was done she waved her hand airily to the staring group and tripped out alone into her own room to dress by herself.

Next, to counteract the unbearable public meals, she instituted the custom of "little suppers." She gave a little supper herself one night a week, to which were invited the royal family and the principal personages of the court. Over this she presided as hostess with grace and humor.

These little suppers came to be so popular that there were soon three a week instead of one. They were proper and dignified. The King invited the gentlemen, the Queen the ladies. And the day after each supper all Versailles would buzz with what the Queen said, to whom she talked, and what she wore. The suppers were a great social triumph for those who were invited. Even the King seemed to enjoy himself.

But one cannot change tradition by a twist of the wrist. The kings and queens of France had stood apart from the rest of humanity for hundreds of years behind the barricade of their etiquette. No one could be intimate with a queen. No queen could act like a human being. As Louis XVI himself said later, when he was looking back on the mistakes they had made: "I didn't know then how dangerous it is for sovereigns to be seen too near. Familiarity destroys respect, with which it is necessary for those who govern to be surrounded. At first the public applauded the abandonment of those old customs; then it looked upon it as a crime."

He was thinking of Marie Antoinette. But in those early days Marie Antoinette threw back her head proudly and prepared to cut down royal life to her own scale.

Her next move was out of the drafty uncomfortable reaches of Versailles and into the charming coziness of the Little Trianon. She could not leave Versailles altogether but she could have at least a spot of her own where she could go whenever she wished to forget the duties and obligations of being a queen.

Little Trianon is an exquisite small palace still standing near the Versailles palace in its own beautiful garden. It is a palace in miniature, a doll's house done in what we now call the "best French taste." Of all places where she lived, this one most nearly expresses the personality of Marie Antoinette herself. Its lovely carvings on panels and doors and ceilings–smiling cupids and garlands of flowers; its colors, cream and cherry and pale blue; paintings by Watteau, the graceful figures of Clodion, exquisite Sèvres plates, fans by Fragonard–in all its adornments Little Trianon is feminine, graceful, sophisticated and lightly playful.

As Queen of France Marie Antoinette had the world of art in her hand–painters, artisans, architects. Her slightest whim produced the most charming furniture, the finest handicraft. It was she who gave the final touch to French decorative art.

Little Trianon was her own, a delightful sanctuary which no one could enter except on the Queen's express invitation. Not even the King would come unless she invited him. Here in spite of reproofs from her mother and warnings from Count Mercy and the Abbé Vermond, in spite of the gossip at Versailles and the distant rumblings farther away in Paris, she played, laughed and listened to music. Never before had French courtiers known such spirited gaiety.

Unfortunately the courtiers who shared this life were few in number. By entertaining at Little Trianon Marie Antoinette was turning a cold—even though graceful—shoulder on Versailles. For the first time in her life she was free to do as she pleased. She was seeing the people she liked to see. She became the Butterfly Queen.

At this time Maric Antoinette was at her most exquisite. She was no longer a child. Her blonde hair had taken on a slightly reddish cast—"cendre," the French called it, "like fire." Her skin was ivory smooth, her arms rounded and young, her eyes large and blue and tender. "Just above the horizon, glittering like the morning star, full of life and splendor and joy," said the Irishman Edmund Burke who saw her at this time.

All the painters of the day vied with one another to paint her. One artist painted her in a rose, another surrounded her with plumes. But what no brush could capture was her litheness. When she ran up the stairs, light as the wind; when she rode—like a very feminine Amazon; when she threw back her head and laughed; when she sat on a sofa talking, leaning forward intimately—she was the most graceful woman in all France. She glided when she walked. "They say she does not dance in time," said Horace Walpole. "If so, time is wrong!"

Every lady in court wanted to look like the Queen. Everyone, even if she disapproved, wanted to have a dress the same color and the same cut as the Queen's. For by now the little archduchess-turned-queen became

Marie Antoinette now became the Butterfly Queen

the arbiter of fashion. Two mornings a week a certain Mademoiselle Bertin, dressmaker, came with her scissors and her thimble and her ideas, and changed Marie Antoinette from a girl who liked plain clothes into the best-dressed lady of Europe. Three months after she was on the throne, the French Queen had become the model of fashionable elegance.

Of course her mother in Vienna heard about it. "I have always held that it is well to be in the fashion to a reasonable extent," Maria Theresa wrote, "but that one should never be extreme in one's dress. A good-looking queen, endowed with charm, has no need of such follies. . ."

But Marie Antoinette was no longer listening.

With elaborate dresses came elaborate hairdressing. M. Leonard, her hairdresser, a very dapper gentleman himself, drove a six-in-hand out from Paris every day to visit the Queen. What he did to her hair and to the hair of all the court ladies is inconceivable today. Hair-dos became so tall that carriage-makers had to raise the roofs of carriages. And on top of the upsweep, as on a stage, M. Leonard would erect a scene of current interest—anything from a popular Gluck opera to a battle scene from the American war then being waged. (The Revolutionary War.)

"They tell me," wrote her mother, "that from the roots on the forehead it rises as much as three feet——!"

But Marie Antoinette tossed her head—as best she could with the weight it bore—and replied that everybody was doing the same. And everybody was, in imitation of her.

Jewels had already been an important part of royal treasure. Marie Antoinette brought many diamonds with her from Vienna. The old king gave her a necklace of pearls, each pearl as large as a filbert nut. Now she scattered jewels across her dresses and through her hair. At one fancy dress ball she wore a black hat trimmed with white plumes that were held in place by a loop of large diamonds. The girdle around her slender waist was of diamonds, and her dress of white gauze was studded with silver stars designed in diamonds. The effect was sparkling and fairy-like. But disastrous for the royal pocketbook.

In January, 1776, she bought a sprig a diamonds that cost 400,000 pounds. In February, a pair of bracelets for 250,000 pounds.

. . ."My daughter, my dear daughter!". . .

The courtiers began to call her "Madame Deficit"—even those who were trying to spend as much money and have as fine costumes as she had.

But no sooner had dazzling splendor reached its height than it began to pall. The queenly fancy now took another turn. This time it was in the direction of simplicity—playful, frivolous and extravagant simplicity, but nevertheless closer to her own natural taste. She made over the garden of Trianon. Trees were brought from all over the world—from Italy, from Arabia, from China, from Louisiana and Virginia. She chose flowers for their fragrance—lilac and jasmine, syringa and orange-blossoms, roses. An exquisite Temple of Love shone white against the green trees of the park. Butterflies fluttered on golden wings; the nightingale sang at sundown.

A brook now trickled among the trees (brought by pipes from many miles away); cows fed in miniature pastures; a mill ground grain. Little farmhouses were added to the picture-book scene, houses made to look old and shabby by cracks painted into the walls, and thatched roofs designed to be prettily untidy.

In this artificial peasant scene Marie Antoinette now changed back to simple dresses of white organdy, and carried a large hat hung by a ribbon on her arm. Again, everyone who could copied her. Among the milkmaids of this theatrical farm village, great ladies strolled as in a play.

(In a sad later day when the Queen's extravagance had caught up with her, there had to be an accounting. The Little Trianon appeared on the top of the list of foolish expenditures, a plaything that cost nearly 2,000,000 pounds.)

As Marie Antoinette simplified her way of living, she made herself increasingly unpopular with a great many of the noble courtiers. They found themselves with less and less to do and nowhere to go. What would a duchess do now who used to hand the Queen her pocket-handkerchief three times a day? How would a duke now occupy himself whose function it had been to walk behind her from one room to another? It was a deep humiliation never to be invited to one of those intimate little suppers, and to hear from others about the gaiety of Little Trianon!

Versailles was deserted. Strangers no longer visited it, titillated with excitement.

At this great distance we can look back and say what *might have been.* If Marie Antoinette had stayed on faithfully at Versailles and tried to adapt herself to its formalities, if she had made herself agreeable to the aristocrats, they might have remained faithful to her. She might have had them rallying to her support in the evil days to come instead of being the first to abandon her.

Grumbling mingled with gossip in the Oeil de Boeuf. The aunts in their dreary apartments now had something to get their teeth into. The court was falling to pieces, and it was "the Austrian" who was tearing it down.

Even then it was not too late. If in spite of scandal-mongering aunts and a core of discontented nobles Marie Antoinette had shown any affection for the common people, *they* would have laid down their lives for her. They truly loved this beautiful Queen. But she was hardly aware of their existence. She was a Hapsburg. She had come from a royal family that placed the monarchy first and the country second.

The "people" as individuals she understood and loved. The disparaging story most often repeated about her has been definitely disproven—the story spread by her enemies that when told the people were hungry and had no bread, she answered, "Let them eat cake!" This was only one of the many false quips turned out by the dozen about her, but one that is unfortunately too easily remembered. Nevertheless as a social obligation she scarcely thought of the people at all.

"I am obsessed by the trouble she may be laying up for herself!" wrote Abbé Vermond.

But the merry Queen tripped lightly and unwittingly along on the crest of her pleasures.

With the arrogance of youth she was impatient with the old. "I don't know why anyone over twenty-one comes to court!" she said laughingly. And the elderly dowagers frowned heavily.

Her great delight was still the masked ball. Nothing pleased her so much as to start off late at night after most of the palace inmates, including her husband, were already asleep, and go to Paris with a few chosen companions, masked and in fancy dress. There she would dance until dawn, presumably unknown. The truth is that her presence was known and fully discussed at every ball she attended. But she was unaware. Once Louis went with her, but as he could not dance and didn't know how to chatter, he never went again. He liked to see his Queen happy, however, so his brother, the Count of Artois, always her playmate, went in his place, as frivolous a young man as a pleasure-loving queen could wish.

What took even greater hold was gambling. This was new to Marie Antoinette and infinitely exciting. She played long into the night—sometimes all night. Though the King did not approve of gambling he gave in oftener and oftener to his charming, laughing wife. The game started after he went to bed and went on through the hours when he was asleep. Marie Antoinette would be just about ready to go to bed herself when he was getting up.

"Let me beg you, my dear daughter, not to give way to this passion. Let me beg of you to wean yourself of it at once. If I do not get a satisfactory answer from you on this point, I shall apply direct to the King in order to save you from greater misfortune. I know so well what consequences will ensue, and that you will lose caste before the public, above all abroad. . ."

But Marie Antoinette had escaped from her cage.

6

Friends and Enemies

It was about this time that Marie Antoinette made friends with two women. For the first time since Caroline left her, she now had real companionship.

One of these friendships started on a very cold day. It was in the winter of 1775–76. The snow had fallen all night and all morning, covering Versailles with a soft white blanket which the wind ruffled and blew in fitful gusts. The villagers huddled indoors around small fires and sent the children into the nearby woods for faggots. The stable boy brushing the shining flanks of his horse put his red hands under the mane to warm them.

For France it had been a bitter winter. But Marie Antoinette, brought up in a colder climate, delighted in it. Remembering Schönbrunn days she now ordered out the sleighs so seldom used in France, and had new ones built. The nobility, some of whom had never been in a sleigh, followed her example. The courtyards of Versailles tinkled with the music of sleighbells. Horses, as pleased as their drivers with the new sport, pawed the ice impatiently.

On this particular day Marie Antoinette and Elisabeth, her fourteen-year-old sister-in-law who accompanied her everywhere, had packed bundles of warm clothing and parcels of food in the sleigh, and were on their way to give them to the poor people who lived in the outlying districts.

They passed other sleighs gliding smoothly over the white road, and sometimes waved their hands. The French princes and noblemen were driving themselves, their horses' heads high with nodding plumes. It was charming and gay and almost as informal as the old Vienna days.

Once they passed a line of low carts heavily loaded with wood moving slowly in the same direction. This was the wood which had been ordered by the King for those in need. "*These* are *my* sleighs," the King once said. But it was not in reproof of his Queen, for he loved her to be happy.

As the Queen's sleigh now pulled up before a small cottage, Marie Antoinette saw another sleigh already standing there, an old gentleman and a beautiful young woman in its back seat. Curly hair and red frosted cheeks peeped out from a fur-lined bonnet.

"Princess Lamballe and the Duke of Penthièvre—," young Elisabeth whispered, "—her father-in-law."

With her usual quick light motions Marie Antoinette threw back her own robes, hopped out of the low sleigh and ran over to the Princess. The Queen knew her as a distinguished member of the court, but seldom saw her because the Princess was in mourning for her husband and rarely joined in any of the gaiety. She had been in mourning for eight years, her husband having died and left her a sad young widow at nineteen.

"You too on the same errand!" the Queen called out when she saw the parcels which the coachman was handing to the old Duke and the Princess.

Princess Lamballe stepped out of her sleigh to bow to her Queen. She was Italian, but unlike most Italians, tall and fair. "Come into my sleigh," said the Queen with spontaneous enthusiasm. "Since we are about the same business, let's do it together!"

But Princess Lamballe could not join her. She preferred not to leave the old Duke alone. Instead she accepted the Queen's invitation to come to dinner the following week at Little Trianon.

Marie Antoinette was twenty, the princess twenty-seven, at the time when they first became really acquainted, and a friendship was cemented at that first little dinner that was to last all their lives.

Shortly after they became friends Marie Antoinette appointed the Princess superintendent of the palace. This was a most important position. It had been abandoned during the previous reign because of the enormous power and influence that went with it. But Marie Antoinette was impulsive and now, as queen, was taking matters in her own hands and making her own decisions. This appointment, to her way of thinking, had two advantages: it pulled the Princess out of her lethargy, and at the same time furnished the Queen herself with delightful companionship.

Actually Princess Lamballe never took advantage of her position. She never tried to use her influence to help out friends and relatives as was only too usual among Versailles courtiers. On the contrary, being wealthy in her own right, she often paid the bills of the Queen and young Elisabeth out of her own purse. No selfish motives ever seem to have entered into her relationship with Marie Antoinette. To see the two young women laughing together in their sleigh, or in spring strolling arm in arm through the Trianon garden, should have made any onlooker happy. But at Versailles there were few unprejudiced onlookers. "Lamballe" was dubbed "the favorite," and in palace politics this meant slander and jealousy.

One night at a ball the Queen saw another face that attracted her attention. Marie Antoinette was sensitive to beauty. One could see it in her home, in her garden, in her furniture, in the fabrics of her dresses. She loved beauty in human beings as well, and for all their elegance the women in the French court were not an assemblage of beauties. The long-nosed sharp-featured agile French were quick and bright and alert. But to the softer, more romantic Austrian they were, generally speaking, not altogether appealing. Marie Antoinette made few women friends in all her years in France. And the two whom she did choose as her intimates were both renowned for their beauty.

The face that she saw at the ball was lovely indeed—a perfect oval, small nose, wide blue eyes in contrast to dark hair, and a gentle mouth. It was the face of Gabrielle de Polignac, Countess, later Duchess de Polignac.

Gabrielle de Polignac was as candid as she was pretty. She and her husband hadn't enough money to maintain a place at Versailles, she said quite frankly when the Queen asked why she never saw her at court. Moreover, Gabrielle added, she did not like the formalities of court.

This was a bond indeed! To find someone else who preferred simplicity to luxury! The Queen at once invited her to come to the palace to live. But Gabrielle demurred. Possibly she hesitated because she truly preferred to live quietly in the country. But more likely, in the light of later events, because her far from well-off family saw ahead of them a practical solution of their troubles. With the Queen's favor they could go far. At any rate Countess de Polignac did not jump at the first invitation, which made the Queen insist harder.

This friendship, even more intimate than the Queen's friendship with Princess Lamballe, had disastrous effects. Duchess de Polignac was indolent and easy-going. What her family asked her to do, she did. When someone wanted a new title, a larger pension, a position in the army, an ambassadorship, she asked the Queen, the Queen asked the King, and in most cases the favor was granted. In choosing Duchess de Polignac as a friend, Marie Antoinette was taking on a huge family with far-reaching connections that grasped for her support and clung like the tendrils of a vine.

Neither Louis nor Marie Antoinette was at ease with the truly important people of their day. When Voltaire, after an exile of twenty-seven years, was allowed to return to France by Louis XVI's order, Marie Antoinette never received him. True, he had too often made France and the French the butt of his satire, and he had chosen freely to live in the court of Frederick the Great. But those near Marie Antoinette believed that her reason for not receiving him was not political. She just didn't know what to say to a man of such giant intellect.

When the Grand Duke and Duchess of Russia came to pay a visit, Marie Antoinette was so confused that she left their presence abruptly and went to her room. "It is even harder to face other rulers," she whispered to her lady-in-waiting, "than to face courtiers!" She took a sip of water, and then went back to the ordeal. With the King of Sweden both Louis and Marie Antoinette were nervous and reserved. And although Benjamin Franklin was living in Paris through much of their reign, the Queen never chose to see him.

She was particularly uneasy with brilliant women. During the eighteenth century women in France were more powerful than in any other time in history. Their influence in worldly affairs was greater than ever before or since. In their salons the finest minds gathered, and there conversation became an art cultivated for its own sake. But Marie Antoinette avoided any contact with these intellectuals. She could never in the world have taken part in their conversations. She had never been educated. She had scarcely even read a book. And she knew only too well what such a handicap meant.

Instead she gathered about her what her brother Joseph called *soi-disant* society, "so-called" society—people who were gay and smart and careless, artistocratic ne'er-do-wells who leaned toward her for support. If one had a favor to ask it was never hard to reach her, the Queen, either walking in the garden, or chatting on a sofa. They told stories, they sang songs, they played games. They went to the races, newly introduced into France by a group of young Englishmen for whom the Queen had a special liking.

The real waste was in her spirit. She was by nature kind and sweet. But her natural kindness and sweetness were devoted to unworthy people. She was young and lively. But youth in her case meant immaturity, and her liveliness proved insatiable.

The price of these new friendships was a nest of enemies. When Princess Lamballe was made superintendent of the palace Countess Noailles resigned her post in a huff. The Noailles were a large powerful family, which now veered over as a body to the growing group of the Queen's discontents. Moreover the outrageous increase in expenses due to the Polignac contingent quite justifiably angered the court which was already piqued by the Queen's independence. Count Mercy, writing later to the Empress, reckoned that in four years the Polignacs had obtained nearly five hundred thousand pounds annually.

Maria Theresa was frantic with worry. She knew that her letters went unheeded now, perhaps were not even read. So she sent an emissary. This was her son, Emperor Joseph II, Marie Antoinette's oldest brother, one who had always been prone to scold, and who now came to Versailles for that express purpose.

It was Joseph's mission to make the French Queen sit up and take notice, and possibly the French King as well. He was not one to soften words or to sidestep an issue. "You are nothing more than an amiable young woman who never thinks of anything but her amusements, her dresses, her daily pastimes. You never read, never hear anyone talk sense for a quarter of an hour during a whole month, never think anything out, and, I am certain, never give a moment's reflection to the possible consequences of what you say or do."

He wrote this to Marie Antoinette shortly before he visited her, with Maria Theresa no doubt dictating. But once he was in his sister's presence he fell a victim, like so many others, to her charm.

To his surprise he also liked his brother-in-law. According to Frederick the Great (a born troublemaker) Joseph had once said: "I have three brothers-in-law who are all contemptible creatures—the one at Versailles is feeble-minded; the one at Naples (Caroline's husband) is a fool; and the one in Parma (Amalia's husband) is an idiot." But he revised his estimate when he met and talked with Louis.

The lasting good of Joseph's visit was that it brought husband and wife closer together. At the peak of Marie Antoinette's folly they had come to see less and less of each other. While she played he slept. While he worked she slept. But that schedule, thanks to Joseph's vigorous advice, was now changed.

Now *everything* was changed. The following year Marie Antoinette gave birth to a child, a little girl, and the royal couple's dearest wish was granted.

What Marie Antoinette and Louis had wanted above all was a child. What the whole country had looked for was an heir to the throne. But the couple had been married seven years, and the people had begun to give up hope. The Count of Artois, younger than Louis, and married after him, already had a son and was secretly nursing the hope that this son would be the next French king. In fact the Count of Artois and his Countess were probably the only two persons in all France—outside the glowering aunts—who were not ecstatically happy at the news.

The little girl, Marie Therese Charlotte, was born December 19, 1778. In those days when a child was born to a queen of France the world was welcome to attend. So, on this day, the room in which the child was born was as full of sightseers as a public park. People even stood on chairs to see better. The crowd was so big and the air so bad and the noise so strident, that the Queen in her weakness had a serious relapse. For a while her life was in actual danger. Such was royal custom in the eighteenth century!

As sometimes happens with the birth of a child, Marie Antoinette's hair began falling out, so she took her hairdresser Leonard's advice and had what he called a *l'enfant* cut—a baby cut. This was probably the first boyish bob, and as usual all the best-dressed ladies copied it. But the Queen was no longer interested in fashion. When Marie Antoinette became a mother, the Butterfly Queen settled down with her wings at rest.

Before Marie Antoinette's second child was born, Maria Theresa died in Vienna. She died November 29,

1780, and her daughter, suddenly released from the dominating personality, was inconsolable. A mighty foundation stone had been pulled out from under her.

The second child was a boy, Louis Joseph Xavier François, the Dauphin of France, born October 22, 1781. This was even a greater happening for the country than the birth of the first child, the little girl. People on the streets threw their arms around one another. Tradesmen from Paris went out to Versailles to parade before the palace, each group with its own band. Chimney sweepers carried an ornamented chimney, butchers brought a fat ox, blacksmiths hammered on an anvil, shoemakers made a little pair of boots for the Dauphin, tailors made him a little suit. Fifty women from the markets came to congratulate the Queen, all dressed in their best black silk dresses. Never, before nor afterwards, was the Queen so beloved by the people of France.

The cultivation of her children's minds now became her first interest. Conscious of her own careless upbringing she determined to do for her children everything that Maria Theresa had not done for her. Dear though her mother had been to her, Marie Antoinette clearly demonstrated that she stood in judgment upon her.

The Duchess de Polignac was made royal governess, and because of the close friendship between the two women, the Queen saw far more of her children than is usual in royal circles. The Duchess now moved into a magnificent apartment in the palace, and the Queen, when she held court, held it there instead of in her own apartments. Here were held the assemblies, the balls, the dinners, the suppers and card parties that were the regular routine of court life. It was another unprecedented change, from which the old nobility recoiled.

Marie Antoinette had curbed her frivolities. She became an earnest mother. The simple people adored her still. But the hostility that had started under her own roof, among her closest associates, was increasing at a dangerous rate. What the aunts dreaded most had come to pass—"the Austrian" was now a beloved wife, a happy mother and an influential queen. It was the end of their own influence on their nephew, the King. The Count of Artois was also disgruntled, as we have seen, with his son no longer a likely successor to the throne. The King's cousin, the Duke of Orleans, was always the Queen's enemy.

"Smears" in the form of pamphlets began surreptitiously to circulate. At first they made fun of the Queen, later they gossiped about her, always they stirred up false rumors. Whence they came no one claimed to know. Knowing herself to be innocent, however, Marie Antoinette disdained to take them seriously. She held her head high and let the lies so maliciously circulated fall about her unheeded. Never was she more a queen.

But a cleverer and more dangerous adversary now stepped into the limelight, a menace not only to the

Queen but to the structure of monarchy itself. This came in the person of tall, elegant, witty Beaumarchais, brilliant playwright who—incidentally—had been one of the most ardent workers in France for the cause of the young American Colonies in their revolution against England.

By 1781 the American Revolution had been won and Beaumarchais turned his critical gaze on the French. In *The Marriage of Figaro* he held the French court up to ridicule. This was the comedy which was later made into an opera by Mozart. There was plenty to ridicule in that already tottering way of life in the foppery, the foolish formality, the extravagance, the selfishness, and the blindness to the needs of the people. The satire was daring and clever, and the King very wisely—for his own cause—refused to allow it to be played.

But he did not forbid his subjects to read it. All the courtiers knew about the edict against a public production, so all naturally wanted to hear it in private. It became quite the stylish thing for a noble to give a party and have a reading of *The Marriage*. The aristocratic guests laughed heartily at their own shortcomings because it was the smart thing to do. "Only petty minds fear petty writings," says Figaro, the barber hero. And none of the elegant nobles wished to be put in the class of petty minds.

By 1784 *The Marriage of Figaro* was played in a Paris theater. The King as usual had not remained firm; moreover, as a gesture toward him the play had been somewhat changed. It had one of the most brilliant openings the Théâtre Français had ever known, and the Count of Provence, the King's brother, sat in the most prominent box.

Up to now the court had been held sacred. Nobles could make fun of each other, but no voice from the outside had ever been raised in public criticism, most certainly not in laughter. With the production of *Figaro* and its enormous success a new power was created—the power of public opinion. The people looked on the court with newly opened eyes.

Marie Antoinette, the mother with two children and another on its way (her third child, Louis Charles, was born in March, 1785) was now a woman of thirty. She was still attractive but no longer a rash thoughtless girl. She took life seriously. But her enemies were gathering, and the four years of fun behind her had cost her far more than they were worth.

The "affair of the necklace," a disgraceful episode in which Marie Antoinette was the innocent victim, showed to what a degree she had jeopardized her dignity. This was a plot that reads like a cheap novel: the intrigue of two rogues involving a fool, and a big swindle. The characters are caricatures, the situations ridiculous. But unfortunately it all actually happened, and its vulgarity has sullied the good name of the Queen of France down to this day.

Jeanne LaMotte and her husband Nicolas LaMotte were the rogues, and Cardinal de Rohan, one of the first

As a mother, Marie Antoinette took life seriously

nobles of France, was the fool. Jeanne was a pretty girl of no scruples who pulled herself up from the gutter, married a man no better than herself, edged her way gradually into the houses of certain nobles, and in time into the palace of Cardinal de Rohan. Her ambition was money and social standing. The Cardinal's ambition was to be first minister of France. He knew that Marie Antoinette disliked him heartily because her mother had before her (he was formerly ambassador from France to Vienna). He knew that with the Queen against him he hadn't a chance of obtaining his heart's desire. Jeanne's game therefore was to pose as the "dear friend" of the Queen, and speak to the Queen for the Cardinal.

Jeanne LaMotte never spoke with the Queen. She never entered her presence. The Queen never knew of her existence. Nevertheless Jeanne claimed that she carried messages to and from the Queen; notes and signatures were forged; and once she and her husband went so far as to arrange a meeting between the Cardinal and the Queen in the garden of Versailles at night. It was of course dark, they had a girl from the streets dressed as the Queen dressed, with a rose, and a note, and very few words to speak.

How the Cardinal could believe such a preposterous set-up is inconceivable. Yet he was completely deceived and deliriously happy to be in his Queen's good (even if secret) graces. But the climax was the necklace. Jeanne, now calling herself Countess LaMotte, told the

Cardinal that the Queen planned to buy a certain magnificent necklace and needed a go-between whose discretion she could depend on, because the King, her husband, must not know. Who could fill this role better than her now good friend, the Cardinal?

Still a dupe, the Cardinal ordered the necklace from the jeweler, and saw it put into the hands of the emissary who was to take it to the Queen.

The emissary of course was Jeanne who then proceeded with her husband to have the diamonds sold one by one, in London, and to live gloriously and recklessly upon the proceeds. They bought a handsome home, had a retinue of liveried servants, a bed covered with scarlet velvet, an English carriage with pearl-gray upholstery, gold plate upon their table, banquets, music, largesse.

But the day came when the jeweler exacted payment. Instead of going to the Cardinal as Jeanne had directed him to do, he went straight to Marie Antoinette in whose possession he assumed the necklace to be. Within thirty seconds of conversation the jeweler knew and the Queen knew that a great hoax had been perpetrated. The swindle was now in the open.

Up to this time Marie Antoinette had tossed her head when people maligned her. But now she was thoroughly aroused and furiously angry. She insisted that the case be taken to court and that every culprit concerned, including the Cardinal, be punished.

If she had been guilty would she have insisted upon a public trial?

Yet as it turned out, the decision to push the case was fatal for her alone. The Cardinal belonged to one of the most distinguished families in France, and the old nobility, already jealous of the Queen's power and enraged by her favorites, at once joined against her in a solid mass. The aunts of course were among them. And the Church took up the Cardinal's cause. Even the Polignacs deserted. At Gabrielle's parties friends of Cardinal de Rohan's were now entertained, which made it impossible for the Queen to be present.

No longer did carriages drive up to Little Trianon and unload laughing guests. The glamor group went elsewhere.

The Queen's name was never mentioned during the trial, but her personality was behind every scene described, and hostility against her—unfair though it was—mounted day by day. Pamphlets carrying the speeches for the defense were circulated by the thousands.

In the end the Cardinal was acquitted, and Jeanne LaMotte sentenced to life imprisonment. But what it really amounted to was that the Queen of France had been on trial before her people. The Cardinal had shown himself her enemy because he had been ready to believe the worst of her. And he had not only been acquitted but had been honored on all sides.

After a few months Jeanne LaMotte escaped from prison and went to England, with whose help is not known. There she was induced to write her "memoirs," false as had been everything else in her life. In them she dragged the name of Marie Antoinette once more through the mire. A new flood of pamphlets worse than any before, all concentrating their venom on the Queen, now inundated Paris and Versailles.

The real significance of the necklace episode is that if Marie Antoinette—during her years of queenhood—had conducted herself with dignity, it never would have occurred. If she had not played with fire, the Cardinal, no matter how foolish, could never have believed her to be a friend of such a rogue as LaMotte, nor would he have believed that she would deceive the King about the necklace. If she had acted with the decorum of a queen, her people would not have listened to the scurrilous gossip that now was passing swiftly by word of mouth as well as by pamphlet from one end of France to the other. Marie Antoinette could no longer toss her pretty blonde head. She buried it in her hands.

7

The Revolution

In 1786 a fourth child was born to Louis XVI and Marie Antoinette. This was Sophie Beatrix, who died before she was a year old.

To Marie Antoinette it seemed as if she had reached

the bottom of the abyss. Her friends had turned their backs on her. She was in disgrace before the people. Her baby had died.

But she was still unaware that the foundations of her world were tottering and that the whole structure would soon fall about her like a house of cards. So far her popularity had been undermined principally in court circles. It had decreased alarmingly by the spread of nasty pamphlets. But so far it had been only a *personal* antagonism. Now the nature of the hostility changed. It became *political* and involved the entire country.

There were some in France who realized that politically their country was headed for disaster even though the Queen did not. Louis XV, the old king, had seen what was coming. "Things as they are will last my time!" he said cynically. But the certainty did not keep him from wasting his life and his country's money.

People outside France saw even more clearly the trouble that lay ahead. "There is nothing to calm my fears in the situation of the king, the ministers, or the State," Maria Theresa had written Count Mercy when Louis XV died.

"Things cannot go on like this," said Joseph II when he visited his sister. "The Revolution will be a cruel one, and perhaps of your own making."

He was the first to say the word "revolution" in her presence in reference to France. But it was not his sister who was responsible, though she was made one of the revolution's earliest targets. The decay in France which brought about the Revolution had started long before Marie Antoinette was born.

The French Revolution shook the world. In years it numbered only five—from 1789 to 1794—the years when France was a bedlam of terror and bloodshed. But it had been a long time coming, and its effects have lasted down to today. The French Revolution changed the way of life of every person in France. It brought about important reforms in nearly every government in Europe. It gave hope and confidence to the poor throughout the western world, and it took away power and privilege from those who had it for centuries.

Those were five terrible years of cruelty, brutality, torture, fear. The people living through the horror could not know what lay ahead, as we know now. Even their leaders lost sight of their first fine ideals and later connived against and spied upon each other. Even they were unaware of how the conflagration started.

The steps that led to this tremendous upheaval seem clear to us now at a distance of more than a hundred and fifty years. But to the people living in France just before the outbreak of the Revolution life seemed to be going on much as it had gone on for their fathers, their grandfathers, and their great-grandfathers.

Most of the countries of Europe at that time, in the eighteenth century, were monarchies. The king and queen, or emperor and empress, or duke and duchess, whatever the rulers' titles might be, had power of life or death over their subjects, the people. These rulers had advisors drawn almost without exception from the ranks of the nobility—their ministers, their generals, their high-ranking clergy. But the people themselves—the farmers, the workmen, the soldiers, the teachers, the shopkeepers—had no say in the government. They had no power whatsoever.

Let us look at France.

France was a rich country. She had big prosperous farms, good roads and canals for carrying the produce of those farms to the cities and to the ports from which it could be shipped, and she had a flourishing trade with foreign countries. For a century she had been the most powerful country in Europe.

Now however she was sliding down hill.

In the first place France's finances were in a bad way. The government was threatened with bankruptcy. Taxation was uneven and unfair. All the world now understands taxation as a burden on all the people. But in France at the end of the eighteenth century the nobility, who owned most of the wealth of the country, were not taxed, and the poor, who had no wealth except that from the labor of their hands, were the ones who paid. It was still not too late—even at the time of Louis XVI—to repair the damage. If everyone in France, it has been calculated, had been taxed just an additional six or seven francs, the "budget" could have been "balanced." The ministers of finance understood the situation. But the nobility were unwilling to make any concessions, and no minister dared stand up against them.

Secondly, there was no social equality among the people. The nobles not only paid no taxes, they also did no work. There were exceptions of course, but as a class they collected money from their estates and spent it in fancy living at court. Even the well-to-do members of the middle class were discriminated against. They could hold no high positions in the army, navy, church or law. To be a captain in the army, for instance, a man had to have four generations of nobility behind him.

Thirdly, the Church offended the people because of the wealth and worldly living of many of its higher clergy—not its parish priests, but its bishops and archbishops and cardinals.

The people of France had many grievances. But it took the American Revolution across the sea to open their minds to the idea of liberty and equality.

Actually the cause of the Colonies was first taken up in France by the nobility. It became fashionable to uphold the downtrodden. It was romantic. Even the Queen supported the American struggle with sympathy and enthusiasm, and gave the ball—in January, 1778—at which the treaty of France with "the United Provinces of North America" was announced.

Benjamin Franklin, who represented the struggling American Colonies at Versailles, was enormously popular. There he was, in his little round hat and plain brown suit, among the fripperies, the laces and the graces of the French court. All France listened to him and many members of the artistocracy, like the young nineteen-year-old Marquis de Lafayette, went across the ocean to fight for freedom. The constitution drawn up by the American colonists was printed in Paris and sold in great quantities. The fact of a people fighting a king for their own independence, as the Americans were fighting King George of England, started the Frenchmen thinking—not the nobility only, or the fashionable Queen, but the plain people of France.

When Louis XV died, these people had looked for a change for the better. As we have seen, they all but worshipped the young Louis XVI and his lovely Queen at the time of the old king's death.

But Louis turned out to be a weak king. He was constitutionally unable to make a decision of his own, and when a decision was made for him, he was just as likely as not, not to stick to it. Any strong-minded person could make him change his mind. He did what the last one he talked to advised him to do. To keep Louis to a purpose was, as one of his ministers said, like trying to keep together a number of well-oiled ivory balls. He was a good man. He wished to help his people. He was not stupid. But he was as unsure of himself as a feeble old man, shaking and unsteady, trying to cross through the traffic of a crowded city street.

Each step in the national drama now unfolding was

gigantic. Every important event of the next five years, and most of the names of the leading figures, are as familiar to us Americans as the events and the names in our own country's history.

The first step was the meeting of the States-General in Versailles in May, 1789. This was a gathering of representatives from all over France—like a big Congress—called together by the King.

The first proposal for such a gathering came from Lafayette. The war in America was long since over, and he had returned to France a hero. But pressure was soon brought on the King from all quarters. Up to now the country had been kept in the dark as to the dangerous financial situation. The people had been deliberately deceived by ambiguous reports from government circles. But now the bad news had leaked out: in Louis' short reign the public debt had been trebled. The people cried out against government perfidy, and because it was something they could point to specifically, they condemned the Queen's extravagances.

As far as Louis was concerned calling the States-General was neither practical nor wise. He was merely shifting responsibility from his own and his ministers' shoulders, to those of the people who had even less experience. But it created great excitement over the entire country and for the time increased his popularity.

The meeting itself was a tremendous event. Two thousand people gathered in the little town of Versailles. They came from all corners of the country to offer their help to the government. They were meeting in the most magnificent palace in the world. Banners were flying, bands playing.

When Louis and Marie Antoinette, dressed in their rich court costumes, entered the crowded hall, the people cheered wildly.

"Long live the King!" they cried.

They cheered their King, but *not* their Queen. "Not one voice was heard to wish her well," reported Gouverneur Morris, the American representative, who was present.

In the period between the affair of the necklace and the meeting of the States-General, "the Austrian," first envied, then distrusted and maligned, had become the victim of popular antipathy. This change of heart had been brought about first by the "evil fairies," the three aunts, then by disgruntled courtiers. Fanned by every kind of publicity, it was bound eventually to reach the world beyond the court. Furthermore, *The Marriage of Figaro* had helped to open the people's eyes. Royalty was no longer sacrosanct. And with that knowledge came an exhilarating feeling of power.

For three hours Marie Antoinette had to sit in front of the people of France, who stared at her with mocking eyes. It was not the last time that she was to appear before them, but it was the last time she ever appeared in her regal robes of state.

To have her people face her in cold hostility was a

frightful experience for the Queen who such a short time before had been loved by all; but it was not as heartbreaking as what she was suffering in the midst of her family. The little Dauphin was very ill. At the opening of the Assembly he was carried in on a pillow. But in a few weeks he was gone. The meeting was in May, and he died June 4th. Louis Charles, the second son, now became the Dauphin, heir to the throne.

The men of the Assembly were not appreciably sympathetic. Their minds were on other matters than a child's death. Even before the little boy was buried a delegation of members came to the King on business.

"Are there no fathers among them?" Louis asked bitterly.

The States-General consisted of 1,200 men divided into three groups; the nobility, the clergy, and the common people—merchants and small landowners—who were now known as the Third Estate.

The Third Estate was equal in numbers to the other two groups combined. But equality stopped there. The Third Estate was separated from the others as sharply as if its members came from another country. In the midst of the silks and satins and plumed hats of the nobles, and the reds and purples of the clergy, it was a solid mass of plain black. These were a people apart—in tricorn hats.

But this discrimination no longer intimidated the Third Estate. If they were to be separated from the upper classes, all right! They would separate to some purpose. A meeting was therefore called, to be held not in the palace, but outside it. This was the famous meeting of the Tennis Court on June 20th. There the Third Estate gave itself the name of National Assembly and drew up a resolution *not to disband until a Constitution for the country had been drawn up.*

The next significant event in the course of the Revolution was the Fall of the Bastille.

Here Louis truly bungled. His first act—of calling the States-General—had been in the interests of the people, even if not entirely wise. Now he made the mistake of shifting to the other side. It may have been Marie Antoinette, or his brother, the Count of Artois, or the last man he talked to, who persuaded him. But he now took a stand *against* the Assembly. He called for a concentration of troops around Versailles and Paris, and he dismissed Necker, the finance minister who had become increasingly popular.

This was the match that set off the flame. To the excited Frenchmen it looked as if calling the States-General had been only a ruse.

The march on the Bastille started at the Palais Royal. In Paris the Palais Royal was the gathering place of malcontents. This was the spot, like Union Square in New York, like Hyde Park Corner in London, where orators roused their listeners, and demonstrations started. It was the sounding board for the liberal intellectuals. Now a slender young man named Camille

Desmoulins, brandishing a pistol, leapt to a table, broke a twig off a tree to make a cockade for his hat, and urged the crowd to violence.

This was July 14, 1789, known now as France's day of liberation. Bastille Day is to France what July Fourth is to Americans.

The Fall of the Bastille was not, however, an entirely glorious undertaking. The people of Paris were frenzied with excitement. Whipped up by Desmoulins, they got guns from the royal arsenal of the Invalides and, thus armed, marched on the Bastille prison which lay on the outskirts of the city. Here they released the prisoners, slaughtered the garrison, and stuck the governor's head on the top of a pike. Flourishing the pike, they marched back triumphantly through the streets of the city.

It was a brutal slaughter because the garrison had already surrendered. Only one shot from an old cannon was fired in defense.

But as a political move the events of July 14th were tremendously important. The people of France had taken a bold step forward on their own. The Fall of the Bastille announced to the other countries of Europe that an age of freedom had dawned.

The Fall of the Bastille terrified the aristocrats. Great numbers of them immediately left France, and by doing so endangered their own cause beyond recall. The nobles who chose to remain at their posts immediately became suspect, and were among the first of the long procession that was soon to be led to the guillotine. If the aristocrats had stayed, their voices in the Assembly might still have brought about more equable results. If they had stayed, the atrocities, the fear, the terror, might have been less. They might even have been avoided. The lives of the King and Queen might have been saved. Who knows?

But once across the border, these *émigrés*, as they were called, went in league with the enemies of France. They did everything they could to upset the new institutions just born. They opposed the freedom of the people and the democratic function of government. Looking back from this distance it seems to have been political stupidity, even if not personal cowardice.

First to leave was Count of Artois, the fair-weather friend of Marie Antoinette in the old days of balls and trips to Paris, and brother of the King. Following soon were the Polignacs. Then the Abbé Vermond, who went to Vienna. The roadways out of France were cluttered with the carriages and horsemen of France's first families. In a mass the so-called friends of the royal couple moved out and left them alone.

The King and Queen did nothing to stop them. In fact they urged them to go. The safety of their friends was now their first concern.

Louis was helpless. He had to send back the troops that he had called to Versailles, he had to recall the finance minister Necker; he even had to wear the tricolor cockade in his hat. This was the red, white and blue emblem of freedom, now become the insignia of the Revolution. It was devised by Lafayette who by now was definitely recognized as a foremost revolutionary leader.

By October another famous milestone in the Revolution was reached. The third important event was the march of the hungry women of Paris on Versailles. That was the fifth of October, 1789.

The harvest had been poor in 1789 and bread was scarce in Paris. Besides this the people were increasingly worked up by the new turn in politics. Any demonstration of defiance would draw a crowd.

Early in the morning of October 5th, a girl from the markets seized a drum and marched through the streets calling on the women to rebel. A crowd fell in behind her, an ever growing mass of shouting people. Wherever the procession approached, stores were quickly closed, windows barred, doors barricaded. "We shall bring back the Queen dead or alive!" the women yelled. "Let the men get the King!"

It was undoubtedly a carefully planned demonstration. Some of the women wore white dresses as for a holiday. Their hair was curled. Men dressed in women's clothes joined them. Gold rattled in their pockets, it is said. But planned or not, it expressed the true feeling of the people of Paris.

The rain came down in torrents as they marched out into the country on their way to Versailles. They were

The hungry women of Paris marched on Versailles

drenched to the skin, and splattered with the mud thrown up by the horses of the National Guard who followed the procession, with Lafayette in command. It was an uneasy Lafayette who now sat on his horse, for matters had gone farther than he had foreseen. Although a confirmed revolutionist, he was not an anti-monarchist. He tried in vain to keep the National Guard back. He harangued his men, but they faced him squarely and refused to obey. Some among them even threatened him. Lafayette was already feeling on his shoulder the heavy hand of the people's power. Already the "moderates" were having to give way to the rabble.

Late that day the mad procession reached Versailles and started for the palace. Most of the Assembly now meeting there were expecting it, including Mirabeau, leader of the Assembly. The only ones who did not know were the King and Queen. The King was out hunting. And the Queen was walking—for the last time—in the pretty garden of Little Trianon. Each hurried back to the palace when breathless messengers came running to them to break the news.

All night the crowd from Paris stayed in the palace, some stretched out on the seats of the Assembly, some lying in the corridors. At dawn a small band of ruffians tried to break into the Queen's apartment, but two very young men who were guarding her held them back. The two youths were knocked down and hit with the butt-end of guns, but one managed to crawl to the door of the Queen's antechamber. "Madame," he cried to a woman inside, "save the Queen!" The Queen was hurried away by a back staircase to the King's apartment while he was going by another way to find her. It was a close call.

The day rose clear and beautiful. France was looking her loveliest as the King, in answer to the calls of the crowd, came out on the balcony and faced the angry, tired, dirty faces below.

The people were not satisfied. "We want the Queen!"

Marie Antoinette had been standing in the room behind, waiting. Now she took her two children by the hand and stepped out.

"No children!" the mob yelled. "The Queen on the balcony *alone!*" Hatred resounded through the clear morning air.

Marie Antoinette had never known fear, and she felt none now. With great dignity she left the children behind and walked out alone. She wore a yellow-striped coat, and her hair was disordered from the terrible night behind her. But she held her head high, and her hands were crossed on her breast.

Her dignity and her fearlessness somehow restored the people to sanity. There was an odd remittance of strength from this woman standing alone, to the crowd below. For the moment they no longer hated.

It was only for the moment. But in that crack of time Marie Antoinette had grown up. She was now a tragic queen. With a woman's intuition she seemed to sense the full extent of that tragedy. When she went back into the apartment she took her little boy up in her arms—now the Dauphin of France—and burst into tears. Through her tears she hugged and kissed him.

The crowd had come to take the King back to Paris. "Sire, you must promise them to go to Paris," one of his ministers advised. Others tried to persuade him and Marie Antoinette to flee. This was one of the times when they could have escaped quite safely had they wished it. Arrangements had been made for carriages to take them to the border. Marie Antoinette had packed her bags and given her jewels to someone for safekeeping. She was ready to go. But Louis could not make up his mind.

The crowd outside shouted, and an occasional shot was fired. But Louis sat there saying nothing. From dawn to eleven in the morning he was the victim of his own indecision.

Finally, at eleven, he gave the word that he would go to Paris. Strips of paper were scattered out over the waiting multitude announcing that the King had capitulated. The Queen insisted upon going with him. They were not to be separated!

At one o'clock the royal family descended the great marble staircase now littered with the remnants of last night's riot, and red with the blood of their defenders. They entered their carriage and started on the journey that was to take them from Versailles forever.

The drive to Paris was one long humiliation. For six hours, on a trip that need take only one hour, the carriage crawled, stopped and crawled on again. Ahead marched the triumphant mob with the heads of two of the King's guard held high on pikes.

The crowd pushed close to get a better view. They shouted insults. "Now we'll have bread!" they cried. "See! We have the baker, the baker's wife and the baker's boy!"

The royal family entered the palace of the Tuileries at ten o'clock that night. To all intents and purposes they were prisoners. If the Fall of the Bastille was not the beginning of the French Revolution, this march, with the mob leading their King and Queen to Paris, left no doubt in the minds of the world.

8

The Flight

It was now Easter, 1791. The King and Queen had been living in the Tuileries palace in the center of Paris since they were brought there—unwilling—in October, 1789. Their two children, the Dauphin, now six, and Marie Therese Charlotte, little Madame Royale as she was called, aged twelve, were with them; also Princess Elisabeth, the King's younger sister, and Princess Lamballe, the Queen's friend. Count Mercy, the old man, came in and out.

It was a quiet subdued household. Madame Royale, a rather plain little girl, made her First Communion, and stayed for the most part contentedly with the older women. The Dauphin, blue-eyed and rosy-cheeked with a gay disposition like his mother's, was continuously asking to go out to the streets of Paris, but it was too dangerous, and he had to walk instead with "mamma" in the garden. The Queen also played billiards daily with the King because he had no other exercise, and embroidered with Princess Elisabeth. Together they made a rug tapestry. At this time Princess Lamballe painted a picture of the Queen—a more serious face now, but alert and alive.

During these two years the few remaining friends of the royal couple had urged them to escape. Three definite well-worked-out schemes had been planned. Marie Antoinette burned with eagerness to go, but the King could not make up his mind to take the fateful step, and she refused to be separated from him.

Even Mirabeau, the leader of the people's party, famous orator of the Assembly and sharp mind of the Revolution, approached them with a plan. To confer with royalty was a delicate matter for a man in his position. Their meetings had to be arranged with strictest privacy for he was already suspect with his party. Mirabeau wanted the King to leave Paris openly and return at the head of his army. But even under this protection Louis could not decide. "The King has only one man near him," said Mirabeau, "and that is his wife."

He was the first of the revolutionary leaders to be won over by Marie Antoinette. But on April 2, 1791, he died. Whether or not he died from poisoning has never been established. Certainly his party had reason to distrust him. And with him went the first and strongest ally of the monarchy among the revolutionists.

On only one subject was Louis firm. That was his Church. He refused to recognize what might be called "constitutional" priests. As the constitution was drawn up there was a rift in the clergy. Those priests who took the oath to the new state constitution were on the side of the new government. They kept their parishes. Those who rebelled and went their own way, picking up a living where they could in the countryside, but remaining faithful as they saw it to their Church, were enemies of the State.

Just before Easter Louis and Marie Antoinette planned to go to St. Cloud, the palace on the outskirts of the city, because out there was one of the old-time priests faithful to the Church. They sent the household servants out to St. Cloud ahead of time. Their dinner was actually being prepared as they got into their carriage to drive out. But the carriage was stopped before they left the Tuileries grounds, their own guard mutinied and refused to go, and for two hours they sat there in the open carriage surrounded by a growing crowd that stared and laughed and made remarks.

In the end they were obliged to go back to the Tuileries where they spent Easter, and where the priest who said Mass was strictly "constitutional."

It may be that this was the last straw. Or it may be that Marie Antoinette finally persuaded her husband to action. Whatever the reason Louis at last consented to consider plans for flight.

This flight was designed by the best minds and reinforced with plenty of borrowed money. But no escapc in history was ever so bungling. Everything went wrong from the beginning, and no one was more to blame than the foolish, inexperienced, painfully innocent royal couple itself.

The details were worked out by Count Axel de Fersen, a Swedish diplomat who was ardently devoted to the French monarchs, particularly the Queen. The party to go consisted of the King and Queen and their two children; the children's governess, now Madame de Tourzel; and the Princess Elisabeth. Mme. de Tourzel was to impersonate a wealthy Russian lady whose passport she was to carry. The two children were to be hers, the Dauphin dressed as a little girl. The Queen was to be the children's governess; the King, the valet; Princess Elisabeth, the lady's companion. Count Fersen was to be the coachman through the streets of Paris.

They were to drive to Montmedy on the border, by

For two hours they sat surrounded by a growing crowd

way of Varennes, where General Bouillé would meet them with a contingent of troops. General Bouillé was one of the few generals still faithful to his King, and besides Fersen was the only outsider in whom the King and Queen had confided.

The royal entourage was to depart secretly and by night.

But what secrecy!

In the first place a special carriage had to be built, one so big that for size alone it would rouse suspicion. But the King and Queen refused to be separated from any members of the family. Six persons therefore had to be driven in the one large "berlin."

Then Marie Antoinette's jewels had to be carefully assembled, wrapped up and sent off ahead. This was done, but not before a spy in the household had told the police. (It was the hairdresser Leonard who carried them out of France for his mistress, and took them to Brussels. Eventually they were restored to Madame Royale.)

Two entirely unnecessary ladies-in-waiting were added to the escaping party, and a number of equally unnecessary trunks. The ladies and the trunks were to precede the larger carriage in a small one of their own.

Another unwise decision was the King's insistence that an escort guard be stationed at each of the relay posts where the horses were to be changed. This was against Count Fersen's better judgment. But—like the big carriage and the trunks and the ladies-in-waiting—

this was a last remnant of royal prerogative. The King and Queen still could not conceive themselves in any other role than that of royalty. They must have a retinue. They must retain this last show of etiquette.

But what was most ridiculous and for them most dangerous was the delay in time.

General Bouillé, on whom everything depended, begged them to make their start no later than June 1st. But they put it off to June 12th, then to June 15th, then to the 19th. Even that was changed at the last minute. A certain serving woman whom Marie Antoinette suspected (and rightly) was to have her day off on the 20th, so departure was put off one more day.

Already there was gossip about a possible attempt to escape. Rumors filled the air. The aunts had fled to Italy in February of that year, making everyone particularly watchful. Emigrés now living in England somehow found out about the plan and talked of it openly. Each month the guard around the Tuileries became tighter and by June was doubled. Lafayette himself paid a nightly visit to the palace to see the King safely in his bed.

Each delay was dangerous, and the final one proved fatal.

On the evening of the 20th all went as usual at the Tuileries. The little Dauphin was put to bed at nine o'clock and Madame Royale at ten, according to their usual habits. The Queen went to the drawing room where she chatted with Monsieur, the King's brother, until nine, when she and the King and Princess Elisabeth went in to dinner. After dinner they separated and went to their own apartments. The Queen was undressed—formally, as always. After the King's undressing—also a semi-public affair—Lafayette came in for his nightly chat.

When everything had quieted down and all outsiders presumably had gone, the Queen got up and crept into her son's room. She took him with his sister to the two ladies-in-waiting, to be dressed. The Dauphin was put into a girl's dress.

"What do you think we are going to do?" his sister asked him excitedly.

He looked down at his "costume." "We're going to be in a play," he said sleepily.

The Queen took the children and Mme. de Tourzel out to the carriage which was waiting. Fersen, on the driver's seat, had been driving back and forth in order to avoid suspicion. Lafayette had passed him but paid no attention.

Half an hour later Princess Elisabeth arrived; near midnight, the King; but they had to wait a long time for the Queen. When she was about to join them she spied Lafayette's carriage still in the courtyard. Swiftly she turned and ran into the maze of paths in the garden, and there, in her excitement, lost her way.

The continued delay became more and more serious.

Fersen was beside the coachman until they left Paris. He wanted someone to accompany them all the way—some faithful friend. But either for reasons of etiquette or sentiment the royal family preferred to go on by themselves.

They were like children. Never in their lives before had they been on their own! Someone had always taken care of them! So now, once they got outside Paris, they showed an unbelievable lack of caution. The King got out of the carriage at the relay stations, walked about, and sometimes even talked to the farmers. He felt safe in his disguise—the round hat and brown frock coat of the valet—and he enjoyed the new freedom from restraint.

Actually there were no newspapers circulating outside Paris in those days, so the people did not know the faces of their king or queen. But there was always the off chance of their being seen by someone who had at one time been in either Paris or Versailles.

The trip was planned for darkness but, owing to a late start, continued into daylight. At each relay station the carriage arrived several hours after it was due, and the guard that was supposed to be waiting dared not wait lest the people's suspicions be roused. Each time the guard was forced to disperse before the carriage arrived.

When they reached the town of Ste. Mènehould, however, what was their relief to find a company of thirty dragoons waiting for them! But the soldiers were surrounded by an excited crowd of townspeople.

"The plans have been badly carried out," the commandant managed to tell them in a low voice. "I must withdraw." And without further words he wheeled his company and departed, leaving the family again alone and unprotected.

The combination of a huge carriage and the unexplained presence of troops caused just such a situation as Fersen and Bouillé had feared. One man in that crowd had been to Versailles. This was the postmaster Drouet, who now thought that he recognized the Queen. He stared at the supposed governess and then at the brown-coated valet. Quickly he got out a coin which had the King's head engraved on it, compared it with the face of the valet, and found them the same. Exultant at his clever detective work he rushed with his suspicions to the mayor, who ordered him to ride after the carriage post-haste.

In the meantime the innocent family rolled along happily unaware of the danger closing in on them. The next stop was to be Varennes, the town where General Bouillé was to meet them with his troops—the last stop but one before they would reach the border, the army, safety and freedom.

When the great lumbering carriage entered Varennes, Drouet, who had ridden horseback over field and through streams, was there ahead of them. He had already spread the news. The bells in the churches had sounded the tocsin (the call to arms), and the Revolutionaries of the region were beginning to gather. No troops were in sight.

But the mayor's representative, Sauce by name, was a kindly man. He was a shopkeeper and he did not like revolutionaries. He stepped up to the carriage as the horses were being unharnessed, but he didn't look in too closely. He asked to see the passports.

All was in order, he declared when he had glanced through them. He was not going to see any more than need be.

But his wife was close behind him. She knew that he knew who the strangers were and she was not going to have her husband thrown to an angry mob.

Wasn't it too late for the travelers to go further, she suggested in an oily voice. They were hot and tired. Would they not spend the night in her home?

The royal party had no choice. The horses had been led away and none harnessed in their place. So they went to the shop of M. Sauce—the King and Queen of France, the Dauphin of France, and two princesses. Wearily and fearfully they climbed the narrow ladder-like stairs to a room over the shop where they were to sleep.

Even then they might have escaped. A powerful friend had followed them with a contingent of horses. This was the Duke de Choiseul who had come behind them all the way from Paris to be ready for any such emergency. He now climbed the ladder-like stairs to make his offer of seven horses. If they left at once, he whispered, before the local National Guard had gathered, they could escape in the general confusion.

As usual the King hesitated. The troops under General Bouillé might come any minute, he said, and when they arrived everything could proceed as planned. He played for time.

It was his last chance, and he lost it. The troops did not arrive. Instead, early in the morning a carriage drove in from Paris. In it were two commissionaries sent out by the Assembly the morning that the royal family's escape had been discovered. One of them, Barnave, had in his hand a decree of the Assembly demanding the arrest of the King.

Now these two men in their turn climbed the ladder to the floor over Sauce's shop, and Barnave handed their fateful paper to Louis.

He read it through.

"There is no longer a king of France," he said sadly and let the paper fall from his hand.

It fell on the bed where the Dauphin lay still asleep. "I will not have my son's bed contaminated!" cried the Queen, snatching the paper and throwing it on the floor.

By now a great crowd had gathered outside. Six thousand persons, they say, were milling about in the little square before Sauce's shop. "To Paris! To Paris!" they yelled.

The royal captives again tried to stall for time, still hoping for General Bouillé.

"We must wait for the children to awake," they said.

"The King is hungry. He must eat."

One of the ladies-in-waiting had an epileptic fit made to order. "We must wait for Madame to recover!"

But neither anger nor pleading nor foolish ruses could hold back the will of the people. The royal family at last descended the stairs and entered the waiting carriage. At seven-thirty they started back for Paris over the roads they had covered so hopefully the day before.

Two hours later General Bouillé arrived at Varennes at the head of a regiment. He had been unavoidably delayed at the border. His horses were now exhausted, and the royal party had already got a big start. He could do nothing.

It was a scorching hot day. The dust was blinding. And the crowds insisted that the curtains of the carriages be drawn up so they could see their prey.

As the King stepped down from the carriage at the Tuileries in Paris there was a deep, amost embarrassed silence. But when the Queen appeared angry murmurs arose on all sides. With head high she entered the palace that she had left five days before. No one should know what she had suffered. All she had the strength to do, once she was back, was to write a word to Count Fersen whose plans for her and her family had so fatally miscarried. "Do not be uneasy about us; we live!"

During those five days it is said that her blonde hair turned white.

An escape was planned but it was so very bungling that after five hectic days the royal family, no longer royal, was captured.

9

The Reign of Terror

The King was now an enemy. By running away he had put himself in a class with the émigrés, and as an émigré he was an ally of the foreign powers that were planning war on France. For ten weeks he was held in the Tuileries and was allowed no part in the government of his country.

The Tuileries became a prison. Members of the royal family were not allowed to talk with one another except in the presence of guards. Sentinels filled the garden and were stationed on every staircase. Two men remained in the Queen's bedroom day and night, before whom she had to undress and try to sleep. Lafayette, general of the Guard, and Bailly, mayor of Paris, were the royal jailers. Even the chimneys were inspected lest the King and Queen try to go up them.

The Parisians were having their fling. But while they were hurling indignities at royalty, like dogs tossing their prey in the air, yapping and barking at it, an event of deeper import and of far greater dignity was coming to a head.

The Constitution which the Assembly had promised to present to the people of France was finished in September, 1791. It had taken 1,200 men two years and three months to draw it up. It was not an easy task—in a country wild with excitement, and under the eyes of the highly nervous Parisians. By way of contrast the American Constitution was drawn up by a handful of very able men who worked behind closed doors in Philadelphia for fewer than sixty days. The Americans pledged themselves to secrecy. The French opened their door to anyone, to applaud, to hiss or argue. The American Constitution is still regarded with veneration after 175 years by a nation more than fifty times the size of the one that adopted it. The French Constitution of 1791 lasted less than two years.

But it was a work of importance, even though it antagonized many. The "Constitutionalists"—the men who framed the Constitution of 1791—may have blundered in many ways because they were inexperienced and over-stimulated. But among them were the truly great minds of France, who saw the white light of freedom ahead. They expressed ideals new to France and to most of Europe—the ideals of Liberty, Equality and Fraternity—those ideals that have come down in history as the direct heritage of the French Revolution.

The Constitutionalists themselves had decreed originally that their period of office should end with the presentation to the people of the Constitution. As things turned out, this proved a disastrous decision. But after two stormy years most of the deputies were weary and glad to go home.

Who then was to put this new Constitution into practice?

Certainly not the nobility, who through it had lost their lands and titles; certainly not the Church, because its power and wealth had also been crippled; not the King, who had shown himself too weak at every step, not the peasants, who now had got the lands confiscated from the nobles and were consequently no longer interested in a new government.

The only group ready to work hard for the new government was the people of Paris, and among them only the politically-minded. These politically-minded Parisians worked through the political clubs, and of all the political clubs by far the strongest and the ablest and the most ardent was the Jacobin Club.

(The Jacobin Club got its name in a roundabout way. Originally a group of Bretons who came to Versailles to attend the States-General met together in a café for discussion. Deputies from other parts soon joined them, and when the Assembly moved to Paris some of these rented a room in a Dominican monastery. The Dominican monks were nicknamed Jacobins—hence the "Jacobin Club.")

The leaders of the Jacobins were Danton and Robespierre, the two names that above all others spell for us "French Revolution."

A great revolution had already taken place. But a monster had risen to guard it, which in the end consumed it.

The first act in the Reign of Terror took place a year after the Varennes flight, in June, 1792.

The night of the 19th of June was soft and warm, the kind of night to stroll along neighborhood streets and chat with friends sitting on their doorsteps, as the people of Paris were wont to do. The people of Paris on this night were certainly out on the streets. No one could keep them indoors. But it was not for lighthearted pleasures. Trouble was astir, and everyone knew it. The air was electric.

In the poor part of the city a small band of leaders had already met in the home of a brewer named Santerre. Whereas the Palais Royal had been the starting point for the early intellectual revolutionists, now the Faubourg Antoine was the nerve center of the strong-arm contingent. The *faubourgs* were the slum sections on the edges of the city, and Santerre, the gang leader so to speak, was "King of the *Faubourgs*." Among his lieutenants who met that night were an American, a Pole, a French marquis.

June 20th was a day that the revolutionists hugged to their hearts. A year ago on June 20th the King and Queen had tried to escape. Three years ago on June 20th the meeting of the Tennis Court had been held.

Now everything was organized. At five in the morning the tocsin sounded. At eight the people of the *faubourgs* began their march from the various corners of Paris. Idlers and loafers joined in on the way, and by the time they converged on the Tuileries the marchers numbered 20,000.

All day this people's army marched in review before the palace, carrying scythes instead of guns, and axes, knives, sabers and pikes until, at nightfall, the gates were broken open and the crowd surged in. The Assembly made no attempt to stop them. Pétion, now the mayor of Paris, knew what was going on but he also did not interfere.

As they were pounding on the wooden panels of the

King's door, trying to break it down, the King gave orders to have the door opened. A band of his faithful attendants obeyed his command and then sprang back to surround him with swords drawn. But he ordered them to sheath their swords; he put on the red hat which one of the crowd took off his own head and handed him; and he stood there—the people's king—for all to see. For three hours he remained standing. He offered no resistance. He didn't even seem to mind.

But for proud Marie Antoinette it was torture. She was not allowed to join the King though she tried many times. Knowing that she was in even greater danger than the King, her attendants drew her into the embrasure of a window and pulled a table in front of her for protection. A group of faithful soldiers of the National Guard stood between her and the crowd now pouring in with Santerre at their head.

"Make way, that the people may see the Queen!" he shouted. Many of them were women, ready to tear her to pieces with their claws. But Santerre held them back. His purpose was humiliation, not physical injury. Humiliation hurt more.

The Queen too had to wear a red hat on her white hair, and one was thrust on her child.

"Oh no!" she protested, as the thick wool cap nearly smothered him. It was her only show of emotion. But she left the dirty cap on the Dauphin's head, his big blue eyes looking out from under it questioningly.

"Madame, the people wish you no harm," said Santerre, reveling in her discomfiture. "No one will hurt you."

Her lips were white with anger. "I am neither misled nor afraid," she answered. "One is never afraid when one is with honest men." As she said this she extended her hand to the member of the National Guard standing nearest, there to protect her. The guard bowed over her hand with deep respect. Her manner was poised and confident. But her arm, when she put it back round the Dauphin, was shaking.

When the crowd had at last satisfied its curiosity and gratified its sense of power, Pétion, the mayor, appeared and told them to go home. When at long last Marie Antoinette reached her husband, she threw herself into his arms and cried.

The next day new crowds came into the garden hoping for a sight of the defenseless King and Queen. The noise of their shouting came in through the open windows. "Is it still yesterday, Mamma?" asked the Dauphin. His usually merry eyes were now frightened.

But June 20th was only a rehearsal.

By now all Paris knew that the King must go. Marat, the little man with the over-sized ugly head, newspaper editor and fiery revolutionist, was inflaming the Parisians to violence: "the imbecile king"—"the perverse queen"—"young whelps of tyranny." The beautiful and eloquent Madame Roland, member of the Girondist party from the south of France which was now the most powerful in the Assembly, spurred that body to take action. Robespierre in the Jacobin Club, and Danton, dark and heavy-browed, waited for the right moment to strike.

But the King and Queen were no longer ignorant innocents. Every motion passed in the Assembly, every argument at the clubs, every distressing item in Marat's newspaper, they knew as soon as the public, and often long before. They now had their own spies everywhere.

The Queen's energy was phenomenal. It was to her, not to the King, that plans for a desperate last-minute escape were brought. But every message that came she took straight to the King. The American ambassador to France was then Gouverneur Morris. He was party to one plan for escape. Lafayette, their old enemy, now entirely on the monarchs' side, had another. He had completed the cycle. Madame de Stäel, also a former anti-monarchist, had a haven ready for the royal family. But the King was apathetic and Marie Antoinette actively distrusted the "turn-coats."

The royal family spent its days in suspense. No one undressed at night, and every time a churchbell rang, they shuddered lying wide-eyed on their beds. It might be the first note of the tocsin. Three or four times during the night the King would go to the different apartments of the family to see if each one was there, and still safe.

"*Êtes-vous ici?*" he would whisper. "Are you there?"

"*Nous sommes encore ici,*" came the answer. "We are still here."

The royal family spent its days in suspense

Marie Antoinette now slept in the room with the Dauphin, who ran over to her bed every morning when he awoke. It was her one happy moment in the day. They kept a little dog with them to warn them of danger.

One morning during that terrible interval of waiting, Princess Lamballe called to her apartment a young Englishwoman who was her own private agent and who had recently become the go-between for the royal family and the outside world. No one knew her name outside the family, and no one knows it even to this day. She spoke French and English and Italian with equal fluency, and she dressed in many guiscs—as milliner's apprentice, as flower-girl, as hawker of jewelry, as fancy toy seller, as perfumer. Most often she impersonated a drummer boy. She was small and thin and had her hair cut short.

Everyone around Paris where people of importance gathered saw her in some guise, but no one except Princess Lamballe knew her in her own character. She carried messages to certain members of the Assembly who kept up a secret correspondence with the Queen, and continued to propose plans for escape. She sent letters in cipher outside the country to Fersen and Mercy and the Duchess de Polignac. Once as a milliner's apprentice she chatted with the dread Danton and walked with her hand upon his arm.

This morning as she waited upon the Princess in her apartment, the door opened and Marie Antoinette and

Princess Elisabeth entered the room. At once our young woman dropped to her knee. Often as she had seen the ladies of the royal family she was shocked now at their appearance. This was the second of August, and since June 20th the Queen might have aged ten years. Her blue eyes were deep-sunk and red rimmed. Both women were haggard from lack of sleep.

Obviously this was a serious occasion. "Her Majesty," said the Princess Lamballe, "wishes to give you a mark of her esteem. She is entrusting to your special care letters which she has written to her family abroad."

Marie Antoinette was remembering the past. She knew that her time might be short and she wanted once more to be in touch with Caroline. She wanted to tell Caroline in her own words of the tragedy that had befallen her little sister Antoine.

She gave three letters to the Englishwoman. One was for the Queen of Naples—that was Caroline. One for the Duchess of Parma—that was Amalia. One for her brother, the Archduke of Milan. Her brothers Joseph and Leopold were now both dead.

"Tell my sisters how it is in Paris," said Marie Antoinette sadly. "Describe what you have seen. Above all, tell them yourself how dear they are to me, and how much I love them." She turned her head away that the others could not see the tears.

The Englishwoman took the letters and left on that very day for Italy. She went to Turin, to Milan, to Parma and to Rome and Naples.

The Duchess of Parma was startled to see someone from Paris. "It is too late! It is useless! They are lost!" she cried when she read the letter. She was determined not to be herself involved. She forced out a few tears, but she sent no answer. It might only commit them all, she said defensively.

With Caroline it was as if the sun shone after a dull dark storm. Caroline kissed the letter. She bathed it with her tears. She could scarcely bear to read it. "Oh my dear, my dear, my dear sister!" she cried out as she deciphered each sentence. "Oh Antoine, Antoine! Why didn't she come to me instead of writing? Tell me all you know—all!"

But the Englishwoman did not know all. Even before she had reached her first stop, the fateful tenth of August had come and gone.

10

August 10th

When you are surrounded by enemies you will try any means of saving your life. Particularly if you are a mother with two young children. Marie Antoinette was cornered. The people of Paris were closing in on her. But she was still fighting.

Some of her mother's political energy had at last been roused in her. But it was too late. Marie Antoinette had never before applied herself to anything practical, and what experience she had in politics had been tarnished by Polignac hangers-on. But because of Louis' apathy she now had to make the decisions alone and make them quickly. If there was to be action she herself had to start it.

To call for outside help at this stage was the most dangerous expedient of all. Yet Marie Antoinette in her terrible distress sent out a cry of despair. She took the irrevocable fatal step.

It was a delicate situation for a French queen. The French émigrés had joined the foreign powers in war against Revolutionary France. At their head were the two brothers of the King, the Count of Provence, who escaped at the time the King got only to Varennes, and the Count of Artois. These two were fighting, not to save France, not to help Louis and Marie Antoinette, but to secure the crown of France for themselves. (This they eventually did. Each brother in turn, many years later, became king.)

A foreign war meant disaster for the King and Queen of France no matter who won. For months Marie Antoinette had written urgent letters to the émigrés and to her Austrian brothers to do everything in their power to *prevent* such a calamity. But on April 20th war was declared, and now that it was an actuality she had to make a choice between the two opposing forces.

On one side was the army of Revolutionary France which she had every reason to fear as a queen. On the other were the armies of Prussia and Austria still in the hands of reigning royal families.

In considering what Marie Antoinette chose to do we must remember an important difference between that day and ours. Up to the time of the French Revolution itself there was no such sentiment as national patriotism. In eighteenth-century Europe loyalty to a country was practically unheard of. Each country belonged to a dynasty—to one ruling family of monarchs. Armies were made up of professional soldiers, not citizens fighting to protect their land. The land itself was the source of food and materials and the wide abode of the people who did the work.

Marie Antoinette's whole soul was devoted to saving her family, not France. As she had been brought up to put the Hapsburgs first and Austria second, so she now put her husband and children ahead of the new French government. From letters unearthed only within the last half century, we now know that Marie Antoinette wrote to the Austrian Ambassador telling him all she knew about the plans and movements of the Revolutionary army—that was the irrevocable step. Today such a disclosure would be considered treason. In 1792 it would have been the choice of any monarch in Europe. In betraying the people's army Marie Antoinette was obeying her natural instinct and the traditions in which she had been brought up.

Her last desperate pleas for help as the chains tightened around her family went out to Fersen. Fersen was in Brussels in constant touch with the Prussian army. Instead of returning home to Sweden he was staying near the French border to do anything that was possible to help the royal family. Between June 20th and August 1st, Marie Antoinette wrote him at least five letters. They were in cipher, written in the third person. She sent these letters concealed in boxes of biscuits, packages of tea, in the lining of a coat or a hat.

On August 1st she wrote her last letter to him. "The arrival of 800 men from Marseilles and of deputies from the various Jacobin Clubs has increased our anxiety. . . For some time they have not taken the trouble to conceal their intention of destroying the royal family. During the last two night sessions of the Assembly the deputies have only disagreed on the means to employ . . . If someone does not arrive Providence alone can save the king and his family."

Fersen was frantic.

The Prussian army under the Duke of Brunswick was assembling near the border of France. For weeks Fersen had been urging the Duke to hurry up his march to Paris. But the general, with German military precision, had insisted upon waiting for all his troops to get into their position. Now Fersen rode hotfoot to demand action in the name of the King and Queen of France. The answer he got was that the Duke would cross the border about the middle of August—in other words, in his own good time.

Fersen knew that it would be too late. So he devised a threat. In the strongest language at his command he devised a manifesto to be sent by the Duke of Brunswick to the French in which he declared that if the smallest violence were done the King or his family, the city of Paris would be handed over to military execution and be destroyed.

This was the "Duke of Brunswick Manifesto" as it was delivered to the Paris Assembly. Paris's reply was to throw the King into prison.

At midnight of August 10th the tocsin sounded. It rang out from the belfries over the rooftrees of Paris, to the ears of those tensely waiting in the Tuileries palace. Underneath the tocsin came the roll of drums, the call to arms. Over all the city, out in the most distant parts, the people rose from their beds.

The King and Queen and Madame Royale, the Princess Lamballe and the Princess Elisabeth, Madame Tourzel and the King's ministers, sat together in the council chamber. No one in the palace slept but the Dauphin.

The Queen had gone to his bedside to say goodnight.

"I want to stay up with you, Mamma," he begged. He was frightened because she was crying.

"I shall be near," she told him, and sat with her hand over his until he slept.

About three in the morning the listening group thought that they heard the rhythmic beating of steps on distant cobblestones. The night was clear and sounds could be heard a long way off. A single shot echoed in the court beside them, making them draw closer together.

The defense of the Tuileries consisted of nine hundred Swiss guards, two hundred courtiers, and a few companies of the National Guard that had remained loyal to the King. These had been strategically placed in the palace and around the grounds by the able National Guard leader, Marquis de Mandat, who saw it as his duty under the constitution to protect his King. But the Revolutionaries feared Mandat's scrupulous integrity. They sent an order for him to appear at once at the Hôtel de Ville (the City Hall) which he ignored, fearing the worst. When a second order came he dared not resist. This was between four and five in the morning.

"I shall not return," he said gloomily. And he did not. Once arrived at the Hôtel de Ville, Mandat was accused of taking measures against the people. He was asked to revoke these measures, and when he refused was sentenced to prison. Even that was not sufficiently speedy. As he was leaving the building a bullet was shot in his head, and his body was thrown into the Seine.

When the news reached the palace that the Tuileries had lost its leader, the Queen at once begged the King to go himself to his defenders—to talk to them, to encourage them, to reassure them.

Because she asked him Louis went forth—Louis XVI, in an old violet coat, with his hair uncombed, his face flushed and his eyes red from lack of sleep. He trudged heavily out to review his troops.

The old courtiers, who would willingly have given their lives to save him, cheered as he passed through the halls of the palace. They had tears in their eyes. Out in the court the National Guards shouted, "Long live Louis XVI!" "We shall defend him until death!" "Let him place himself at our head!" "Down with the Jacobins!"

But the King had no words ready with which to reply. He was grateful, but he hadn't the spirit within himself to give them heart. Had Marie Antoinette been there instead she could have spurred them to action, for the effect of her personality was electric. But not Louis'.

As he went farther from the palace itself the cries changed in tone. "Long live the nation!" came now, instead of "Long live the king!"

Still farther, the crowd gathered outside the walls hooted when they saw him.

Marie Antoinette, still in the council chamber, had been listening sharply. She heard the outside yells. "All is lost!" She shook her head. "He has done more harm than good!"

By the time Louis returned the sun had risen blood-red in the eastern sky. The shouts rose in volume as the crowd got bigger. "Deposition or death!" came to the ears of the listeners in the council chamber.

Municipal officers and the commander-in-chief of the Guard and the public prosecutor, Roederer, tried to quiet the crowd. But they were outshouted. Again Pétion, the mayor, whose duty it was to keep order in the city, had long since abandoned the palace and retired to his own home, where he stayed all day.

By eight o'clock things looked so dangerous that Roederer begged the King and Queen to take refuge in the Assembly which was then meeting in the old riding school of the Tuileries.

The Queen refused proudly. To ask shelter of the Assembly whose members had done nothing to prevent the riot, who went on with their endless debates and arguments while the monarchy was writhing in its death struggle—that indeed would be abdicating! "You can nail me to these walls before I shall consent to leave!" she cried in her bitterness.

The King stood silent.

"Sire," the public prosecutor addressed himself to the King, "time presses. We no longer entreat you. There is only one course left for us: we beg permission to carry you off by force!"

Louis raised his head and looked closely at Roederer with his weak eyes. Then he nodded his consent.

The Queen of course had to give in.

Slowly they marched out of the palace. The King

was in front alone. The Queen followed with the Dauphin. Then came Princess Elisabeth and Madame Royale, Princess Lamballe and Madame Tourzel, and behind them the King's ministers, and a few faithful friends—"the funeral train of royalty."

The crowd through which they passed was keyed up to the point of fury. "Down with him! Don't let him enter the Assembly!" "No women! We want only the King!"

A guardsman seized the Dauphin in his arms and the Queen cried out in terror. She thought he was carrying the child off, but he was only trying to protect the child from the mob.

With the National Guard holding back the crowd as best it could, the royal procession finally entered the Assembly. But not before someone had stolen Marie Antoinette's watch and purse.

The royal family was out of the palace just in time. Behind them they could hear shots. Fighting had already started in the Tuileries.

They were put in a tiny room usually used by the news reporters. It was ten-foot square and open to the hot sun. Here they stayed crowded together for seventeen hours.

In the meantime the people's army had entered the palace and ordered the Swiss guard to surrender. In reply the Swiss shot a volley into their midst and scattered them in every direction. It proved at least that a few disciplined soldiers could even then have held the ter-

The royal family vacated the palace just in time, for

fighting had already started in the Tuileries

rorists down. But the King, from his ignominious position, was still giving orders. He now sent word to the Swiss guard to cease firing, to evacuate the palace and to lay down their arms. Although such an order was not inconsistent with Louis' love of peace and his dread of bloodshed, it may have been inspired by his jailers.

It was at this point that a young soldier with a military turn of mind stood outside the Tuileries watching the fighting. Being out of a job he had nothing better to do. Many years later he gave his opinion of that morning's fiasco: *a few cannon shots, a vigorous sally, and the mob would have been swept away like leaves by a broom.* The young soldier was a Corsican named Napoleon Bonaparte.

After the Swiss guard had laid down their arms, the people's army, headed by the troops from Marseilles, rushed into the palace and made it their own. They sang the song which the soldiers from the south were singing when they entered Paris—the *Marseillaise:*

"Ye sons of France, awake to glory!
Hark! Hark! the people bid you rise!
Your children, wives and grandsires hoary
Behold their tears and hear their cries!

"To arms, to arms, ye brave!
The avenging sword unsheathe!
March on! March on!
All hearts resolved
On liberty or death."

Its strains resounded across the garden to the ears of the wornout King and Queen. They have resounded down through the years to us—as the song of release for the oppressed and of liberty for all.

For seventeen hours—from ten in the morning to nearly three o'clock in the night—the royal family sat, and their little group of devoted followers stood, in the hot room outside the Assembly. The Dauphin had fallen into a heavy sleep and lay on his mother's lap dripping with perspiration. She tried to wipe his face with her handkerchief but it was too wet and she had to borrow one from the Count La Rochefoucauld who stood near by. The handkerchief which he gave her was stained with blood.

Blood was everywhere. The floors of the palace were slippery with it. Red footprints marked the path.

They saw the treasures of the palace brought in and thrown on the tables as so much loot. Furniture had been broken up, mirrors were shattered, wine cellars opened up. The Swiss guard, unarmed, were assaulted, mutilated, murdered.

After the Marseillais troops had had their way in the palace they appeared at the Assembly. There they demanded that the King be deposed.

The Assembly bowed to force. A proclamation depriving the King of his powers was read by the president, and the National Assembly declared itself the sole legislative authority of the State from now on.

On August 13th the family, no longer royal, was removed to the Temple, an austere fortress 600 years old. All but the immediate family were ordered to withdraw separately. When the friends and ministers knew that they were to be parted from their King, perhaps forever, each as he passed by put all the money he had on a table. They knew that the King and Queen had nothing.

"Gentlemen, keep your pocketbooks," said Louis gently. "You have, I hope, a longer time to live."

Marie Antoinette still fought to save the royal family, but all was in vain. All hope ended when a violent mob on August 10, 1792 stormed the Tuileries, where the royal family were prisoners. The people then demanded the Assembly to deprive king of all powers.

11

The Guillotine

It was probably Danton who organized the attack on the Tuileries, who had the Swiss guard hacked to pieces, and delivered the King and Queen to captivity. Danton was a patriot. He destroyed the monarchy because he believed that what France needed was a

working republic. He governed by fear because he considered the cause desperate.

Danton was a statesman who used fiery weapons. He was a man of great size with savage mouth and intense eyes under dark overhanging brows. His powerful voice frightened his listeners and spurred them to action. He shouted, he raged, he swore. But through it all he kept an extraordinary balance of mind. "To conquer, we must dare, and again dare, and without end, dare!" he thundered. He was selfless. "Let my name be blotted out and my memory perish, if only France be free!"

Under him the Terror grew in fury. It is said that only one out of a hundred and thirty Parisians was an active supporter of the Terror. The brains of the movement, as in nearly all revolutions, were centered in a small tight group of fanatics—in this case the Jacobin Club; but their supporters, even if only one out of a hundred and thirty, were made up of irresponsibles, already mad with murder. This dangerous army of the riffraff was swollen with its own feeling of power. All it needed was the word to go.

The word came in September. The Prussian and Austrian armies had now entered France and at the first clash had sent the Revolutionary army running. Longwy fell, and the great fortress of Verdun. Lafayette fled from his post with the army and crossed the border to Liège. On August 19, 1792, he was declared a traitor by the French Assembly, and ironically—as a

leader of the rebels—he was held prisoner by the Prussians and the Austrians for five years.

As the enemy continued to advance toward Paris the government was obsessed by fear: with the invading army to back them up, the royalists, the constitutionalists and the clergy would join forces, rise against the citizens, and try to restore the old order!

"Treason" was whispered through the streets and alleyways of the city. And "suspects." Anyone was a "suspect" who might conceivably have aided the enemy, and all "suspects" were to be destroyed. The whisper rose in volume as it reached the *faubourgs*. It had the compelling fury of a witch hunt or a lynching.

When the crowd was at fever pitch a signal was given for the prisons to be opened. One by one the prisoners were led from their cells, questioned briefly, and either pardoned at once or thrust out to the mob impatiently waiting at the gates. There they were hacked, stabbed, their heads cut off and stuck on pikes, and, as was revolutionary custom, carried through the streets. In three days and nights of that first week in September, 2,000 prisoners were killed. This was the warning, violent and bloody, deliberately planned to strike fear into royalist hearts.

The prisoners in the Temple knew nothing of these desperate events. They had no communication with the outside world and very little with each other. They saw no newspapers. Their guards were instructed to tell them nothing.

But they did hear the distant tocsin on those September days, and the wild shouting that brought back to them terrifying memories of Versailles and the Tuileries. Paris was on a rampage. On the third day the shouts came so close that they seemed to be surrounding them. The prisoners saw that the faces of even their rough guards paled.

Princess Lamballe had been among those prisoners murdered. Her head had been cut off and the ruffians now surrounding the Temple held it high on a pike for the Queen to see. The head was still beautiful with its long curly hair hanging loose.

In the history of the Revolution this period is known as "the September massacre."

On September 21st the Assembly formally abolished the monarchy. The King was legally deposed. To all intents and purposes he had been deposed on August 10th when they brought him to the Temple; on June 20th he was already a prisoner of the people; and for the three long terrible years since he and Marie Antoinette and their children had been forcibly removed from Versailles he had had no kingly power or prestige. But now he was Louis the Last. He was Louis Capet. (Capet was the family name of the old French kings.)

The Revolutionists had deprived the King of his powers. They had taken his crown. What next?

On December 11th, Louis XVI was brought to trial before the National Convention. For six weeks, while the trial lasted, he was allowed no communication with his family though he still lived in his own room in the Tower of the Temple and they above him.

Marie Antoinette begged the guards for news of him. But when she finally heard it, it came from the outside through the closed windows. On January 20th the news venders were shouting through the streets that the King had been condemned to death.

That night Louis was given permission to see his family—his wife, his children, his sister. It was the King's farewell to his Queen—the pert pretty girl he had met so shyly in the woods of Compiègne twenty-two years before, the girl he had been afraid of, but whom he had come to love and cherish. Their farewell was not in private. A glass door separated the family from the guardsmen who watched the scene with curious interest: Louis talking solemnly to his little eight-year-old son and the child raising his hand as if taking an oath. (The King made the little boy promise not to try to avenge his father's death.) The women scarcely spoke. It was like a tableau to those outside—the family standing there in their helplessness and sorrow.

At ten o'clock Louis told them to return to their own apartment, and promised that in the morning he would call them for their final meeting. He needed now to pray.

All night long Marie Antoinette did not undress. Toward morning she heard sounds below: it was her husband about to call her! But no steps approached her room. Before long she heard the sound of carriage wheels on the stone paving of the court, and she knew that he had gone. It was by Louis' own order that she was not called. In his gentle kindness he wanted to save her the agony of a last farewell.

Louis XVI—Louis Capet—was led to the guillotine in the Place de la Révolution by Santerre, the brewer. Louis stepped firmly and resolutely up the steps of the scaffold. "Frenchmen," he said, "I die innocent of the crimes which are imputed to me; I forgive the authors of my death, and I pray that my blood may not fall upon France." He was still speaking when Santerre ordered the drums, and their rolling drowned out his voice.

Marie Antoinette was now the Widow Capet, a prisoner in the Temple with her children and her sister-in-law Elisabeth. The guards who surrounded her were rough men—men from the dregs of Paris who, as the Revolutionaries figured, were right and proper guards for royalty.

But the Revolutionaries had not reckoned on the quality of pity. One of the guards was a man named Toulan, a man so ardently revolutionary that he had been one of those who volunteered to storm the Tuileries on August 10th. It was because of his strong anti-monarchistic convictions that he had been especially picked to guard the Queen.

He watched her now in the Temple. Her hair was

white and she wore an ill-fitting black dress of mourning which the Assembly had allowed her. She had her children beside her constantly. There was a small harpsichord in the room which the Princess Elisabeth sometimes played. Marie Antoinette had taught her young daughter some songs which she often sang to her aunt's accompaniment. To hear singing in the prison, to see this woman so very sad and so hopeless still trying to bring some lightness into her children's life, gave Toulan a glimpse of a new kind of life. He found himself wanting to help her.

There were also some faithful Royalists still hidden here and there in Paris. They had money. They too wanted to help. Even at this bitter end the Queen was not without friends.

One of the most active of the Royalists was the Baron de Batz, a man of great wealth and mad courage. The Revolutionaries knew him to be a dangerous daredevil and they were sure that he was hiding in Paris. He was listed in the files of the secret police with a price on his head. But he could not be found.

The Revolutionaries were powerful. But De Batz was too sly for them. While they were hunting him in vain he was living safely in the home of one of their most trusted comrades. Cortey, a grocer, was at heart a royalist. But in the organization of the Revolution he was the military commander of this section of Paris, and the guards of the Temple were under his supervision. What better companion could De Batz find?

So—through the sympathetic clean-hearted Toulan, through Toulan's friend, the lame schoolteacher Lepitre, through the grocer Cortey, through De Batz, and by his money through the inspector of prisons, Michonis, who could be bought—a scheme to save Maria Antoinette and her children was devised that is one of the startling melodramas of history.

First, the Baron de Batz got himself enrolled as a private in the Temple guards. In this capacity he was able to learn the layout of the building. Briskly he trod back and forth in front of Marie Antoinette's door when on duty—back and forth, an aristocrat unrecognizable in his ragged uniform. In his off-duty hours he was lining up his reserves and perfecting his plans.

When the final night came, a company of thirty men was on guard at the Temple, every one of them a Royalist, including their leader De Batz. Under military commander Cortey they marched smartly into the Temple grounds, and were placed by Cortey in strategic positions in the Tower, on the staircase, in the halls. Michonis, the inspector of prisons, was on guard in the apartment of the princesses. His part in the scheme was to open the door for the prisoners and throw large military cloaks around them. Looking thus like soldiers and carrying weapons, the three royal women were to step into one of the groups of De Batz guards already standing there, and in their midst the young Dauphin, now King Louis XVII, was to be hidden. This patrol was then to be led out of the prison by Cortey, who, as military commander, was the only one privileged to open the large gates during the night. Outside everything was ready for a quick departure.

This was the set-up, all carefully worked out, for that night in the Temple.

Suddenly at eleven o'clock came a loud banging on the outside door. It was Simon the cobbler, a member of the Revolutionary Commune, who came bursting in, crying out that the Queen was escaping.

Who betrayed them no one ever knew. But the instant Cortey saw Simon he knew that the game was up. On the other hand, the sight of Cortey reassured Simon. "If *you're* here it must be all right," said Simon with relief.

But Cortey was taking no chances. With a quick order he got his detachment of thirty men under way and ordered them to proceed out of the Temple gates. These were the thirty Royalists with De Batz.

In the meanwhile on the floor above, Michonis, who was an easy talker and always master of the situation, took the offensive himself and instead of cowering or explaining, began to scold Simon. Later he went so far as to denounce Simon to the Commune, and was himself completely exonerated.

In this way all the conspirators were saved. But the Queen remained—a hundred times worse off than before.

Way over in America the Queen had more friends. In the town of Azilum on the Susquehanna River, a group of French émigrés built a huge log house to receive her, but it took news so many months to travel from Paris to Azilum that when the émigrés were just beginning work on *La Grande Maison* their Queen had already died.

Even if Marie Antoinette had escaped, the course of history would have swerved only a little. This woman, once so brilliant on the stage of Europe, was only incidental in the great surge toward freedom and social equality that was sweeping across the continent. She was soon to be almost forgotten in the bloody progress of the Revolution.

But at the moment Paris still had her in its hands.

And the people of Paris were keyed for revenge.

Louis XVI was dead. But Louis XVII was still alive—a little boy, so often disturbed by his mother's tears. Now on the third of July they took him away from her.

It happened about half-past nine at night. Elisabeth was reading aloud, Marie Antoinette was mending, her daughter sat at her knee listening, and the boy was asleep, when the door burst open and six men entered without knocking. They were officers of the municipality. "We have come to take the son of Capet," they said.

"No!" cried Marie Antoinette and like a lioness sprang between the men and the bed. She rarely protested. Her pride made her endure the deepest humiliation in silence. But this was the mother, not the queen.

The little King awoke and cried. She pleaded. But these men were not moved by pity.

The child's aunt and sister dressed him because his mother was too unnerved, but she gave him a last kiss and held him close in her arms. As the men led him down the hall she could hear his cries as he struggled against them—far down into the depths of the Tower.

Now they were three women alone.

The boy was put in the care of Simon, the same shoemaker. Marie Antoinette knew because through a tiny window in her closet that opened on to the stairs, she one day caught a glimpse of Simon taking him up to the platform on top of the Tower. No longer did the child wear mourning as a young prince would wear for his father, but the red cap of the Revolution. Simon, being a rough man, treated him roughly. Every day he took him up. Every day it was a fresh wound opened. But the mother had to look out through that crack!

One by one those whom she loved were taken away. On August 2nd Marie Antoinette herself was removed from the Temple and sent to the Conciergerie. This was the small prison in the ancient Palace of Justice. It meant that her turn had come.

Her cell at the Conciergerie can still be seen as it was then. It is below the level of the street and when the waters of the Seine are high the walls drip. It was always damp and cold. The floor was of bricks and there was no heat. For furniture there were two chairs, a cot, and a table. There were no curtains, the sheets were gray and coarse, and the straw mattress was torn. The guards assigned to look after her were issued the same kind of cots, but they complained and received others. Three persons—a waiting woman and the two guards—slept in the cell with her, all on new cots. But not the Queen. She was not permitted to have wool or needles with which to knit. Once in a while a guard, sorry for her, brought her a book, and for the first time in her life Marie Antoinette was driven to read.

More than one was sorry for her. The same Michonis, as inspector of prisons, came to see her often. Toulan communicated with her by signs and took messages to Elisabeth and Madame Royale at the Temple. The concierge and his wife, Mr. and Mrs. Richard, did what they could.

In the market one day Madame Richard was looking for the nicest melon. It was August and melons were ripe.

"I know for whom," the melon vender said, shaking her head. She too searched for the best. "Keep your money, and say to the Queen," she whispered, "that there are among us those who are sad." Perhaps she was one of the market women who went out in black silk dresses to compliment Marie Antoinette on the birth of the first dauphin. Maybe she was one of those who joined the hungry women and marched out to Versailles to hurl insults in October, 1789.

The concierge saw to it that the Queen's food was good even though she could scarcely eat. At least it was wholesome.

It was now October and the water trickled down the walls and gathered in small pools on the floor. To keep off some of the dampness he hung an old carpet around her bed.

The prison inspectors at once accused him of softness toward the prisoner.

"Don't you see that it is to break the sound so she can't hear what goes on in the next room?" he asked with sham indignation. They agreed that he was right.

Now the women in the market began to send in grapes.

The Austrian army had crossed the borders of France. Count Mercy begged the Prince of Coburg, general-in-chief of the Austrian army, to direct a body of cavalry to Paris to save the Queen. "Can posterity believe that so great a crime could be committed at just a few days' march from the victorious armies of Austria, and those armies make no effort to prevent it?"

The Austrians were forty leagues from Paris. The condemned Queen of France was the aunt of their emperor. But not the slightest effort was made to save her.

The day of her trial was October 12, 1793. True to her feminine instincts Marie Antoinette tried to look her best for that important occasion. Her short white hair was carefully arranged and to her little cap she added two ribbons from which hung black mourning crepe.

The trial is on record and her answers have come down through the years, simple, dignified, accurate. "Marie Antoinette of Austria, thirty-eight years of age, widow of the King of France. . ." For fifteen hours the tribunal questioned her and she answered. Nothing was achieved except that she was exhausted. When she asked at the end for a glass of water no one in all that crowd of people was brave enough to get her one.

Finally the officer of the guards who was assigned to escort her back to her cell gave her a drink of water. This was a man named De Busne. On her way to the cell she had a dizzy spell. "I am exhausted," she told him. "I cannot see. I cannot walk." So he offered to support her, and she took his arm.

The next day De Busne was arrested and convicted as a counter-revolutionary spy. The Revolutionaries were afraid of their shadows.

At the trial Marie Antoinette was given two defenders, lawyers called by the government to give a semblance of correct legal procedure. These men were as decorous as are all trial lawyers to their client. "How tired you must be!" she said at the end of the second long day when they had summarized their defense.

Her words of commiseration were heard, and both men, before her eyes, were arrested.

The jury was unanimous in finding Marie Antoinette guilty as an enemy of the state. And Fouquier-Tinville, the Public Prosecutor, asked for the death sentence.

When the sentence was read the judge asked the routine question: had she any objection to make to the application of the sentence? She shook her head. There was no sound, no gesture, no tear. She walked from the hall with her head erect, and returned to the Conciergerie where she was put into the cell of those condemned to death.

The pretty little archduchess, the fun-loving dauphiness, the butterfly queen, was now a woman. Alone in her cell at the Conciergerie she wrote a letter that only a woman of character and wisdom would have penned. It was to Elisabeth who had up to now shared her tragedy. The letter is dated October 16th, at half-past four in the morning:

"It is to you, Sister, that I am writing for the last time. I have just been sentenced to death, but not to a shameful one since this death is shameful only to criminals, whereas I am going to rejoin your brother. Innocent like him, I hope to show the firmness which he showed during his last moments . . . You who in the kindness of your heart sacrificed everything to be with us—in what terrible position am I leaving you! I learned during the trial that my daughter has been separated from you. Alas, poor child, I dare not write to her; she would not receive my letter. I do not even know if this one will reach you. But I send them both my blessing in the hope that some day, when they are older, they will be with you once more and will be able to enjoy your tender care . . . May they both feel that whatever their situation they will never be truly happy except together! Let them take pattern from us! How much consolation our affection brought us in our misfortune! I hope my son never forgets his father's last words: *Let him never try to avenge our death!* . . . I here bid farewell to my aunts and to my brothers and sisters. I had friends. The thought of being separated from them forever and of their distress is among my greatest regrets in dying. Let them know at least that in my last moments I have thought of them. . . . Adieu, my good and affectionate sister. I trust that this letter will reach you. Think of me always. I send you my most heartfelt love, and also to my poor dear children. How heartbreaking it is to leave them forever! Adieu, adieu. I must now devote myself entirely to my spiritual duties. . . ." The letter ended abruptly.

Even the handwriting is strong and firm, not the childish unformed letters of other days. She was indeed a woman.

(This letter never reached Elisabeth. Twenty-one years later it was sold by a man who had saved it to make a profit. Princess Elisabeth was guillotined in May of the next year. What happened to the Dauphin is not certain. Either he perished in the Temple, or he

Marie Antoinette rode to the guillotine in a tumbril

lived out his life elsewhere under another name. No one knows.)

At five in the morning the call to arms was beaten in the forty-eight sections of Paris. By seven all the military forces were out. Cannon was placed on all the nearby bridges, and a cordon of 30,000 soldiers lined the way from the Conciergerie to the Place de la Révolution.

Masses of people crowded around the entrance to the Conciergerie, and a murmur like the waves of the sea spread out over them when at eleven o'clock the gate opened and the Queen stepped out.

She wore a loose dress with a fichu of white muslin around her neck. On her head was a linen cap, and on her feet were black slippers with high heels. She was tall and thin and straight. She looked a queen.

Louis had been driven to his death in a carriage. But for Marie Antoinette there was only a tumbril—a rough cart with a plank for a seat, pulled by a white horse. The Queen sat with her back to the horse and behind her stood the executioner, Samson, holding her elbows back by a cord.

The cart moved with terrible slowness through the crowds of men and women. They were not all shouting. It is said that many fainted, and many wept at a woman's humiliation.

Marie Antoinette climbed the steps of the scaffold without help. In doing so she stepped without meaning to on the hand of Samson, the executioner. He gave an involuntary cry of pain.

"I beg your pardon, Monsieur," the Queen said, polite from force of habit. She had been badly brought up for the important things in life, well brought up only in the small amenities.

At a quarter past twelve, October 15th, Marie Antoinette was guillotined and the once proud head was held high by the executioner for the people to see.

"Long live the Republic!" resounded across Paris.

On September 21st after 'September massacre' the Assembly formally abolished the monarchy, and legally deposed the king. Six weeks later Marie Antoinette's husband (of 22 yrs.) went to the Guillotine. The next year her son was separated from her and finally she went to trial Oct 12, 1793, and was found guilty. The pretty little archduchess, the fun-loving daupiness, the butterfly queen was now a woman who rode to the guillotine in a tumbril cart on October 15, 1793. "Long live the Republic!" resounded across Paris.

Postscript

Marie Antoinette was soon forgotten, so trifling small is the death of a queen in the great task of making a new nation.

For eight months more the Terror continued, with the Jacobins firmly in the saddle. The final triumph of the Revolution was due to their fanatical devotion; and to the triumph of the Revolution France owes her place in the modern world.

Robespierre was their leader, a little man only a bit over five feet tall, with a receding forehead and pale face pitted with smallpox. His eyes were weak and he wore spectacles. For eight months more he was the ruler of France. He was a ruthless leader and his government the most autocratic ever known up to that time. But together they saved France. It was a national government, no longer a monarchy, and in a great outburst of patriotism the young men of the country flocked to the army. It was this inspired army that defeated the foreign and émigré armies closing in around France—the same army that Napoleon later led to victory.

Inside the country the new government under Robespierre learned how to govern. The political business was now carried on in the rooms and halls of the Tuileries amid bronzes, clocks, mirrors and tapestries dilapidated from the frenzy of June 20th and August 10th. Where the King and Queen had played billiards such a short time before, where the Princess Elisabeth embroidered with the Queen, where the Princess Lamballe painted her portrait—here the committees worked at their grim orders of the day. From early in the morning until late at night these men of Paris toiled. In the garden where the Dauphin ran happily into his mother's arms, sentinels picked from the markets now tramped up and down armed with pikes.

Every night at ten o'clock came the toll. This was the hour when the public prosecutor came to announce how many persons had that day been convicted by the Revolutionary Tribunal, how many acquitted, and how many taken away in the tumbrils the night before.

Only a stone's throw away from where they sat was that huge black monster, the guillotine.

Whose head would fall next?

Most of the persons whom we have met in these pages were beheaded: revolutionary leader Barnave,

General Bouillé, both connected with the flight to Varennes; Countess Noailles, "Madame Etiquette"; Leonard the hairdresser; beautiful Madame Roland and the other Girondists of the Assembly; even the guards of the Temple, Toulan and Lepitre, who tried to help the Queen, and Michonis, the inspector of prisons. Danton's head fell under Robespierre's orders, as did Desmoulins', who started off the mob to the Bastille. Two thousand, six hundred and sixty people were guillotined, most of them under Robespierre's cold weak eye in the last four months of his rule. Then the Convention in turn destroyed him.

On July 28, 1794, Robespierre himself was guillotined. And the Reign of Terror was ended.

Out of revolution, France emerged an organic nation.

Index

Index

Index

Index

Index

Index

Have you read these World Landmarks?

★

CHECK THE LIST BELOW

W-1 **The First Men in the World,** by Anne Terry White

W-2 **Alexander the Great,** by John Gunther

W-3 **The Adventures and Discoveries of Marco Polo,** by Richard J. Walsh

W-4 **Joan of Arc,** by Nancy Wilson Ross

W-5 **King Arthur and His Knights,** by Mabel L. Robinson

W-6 **Mary, Queen of Scots,** by Emily Hahn

W-7 **Napoleon and the Battle of Waterloo,** by Frances Winwar

W-8 **Royal Canadian Mounted Police,** by Richard L. Neuberger

W-9 **The Man Who Changed China,** by Pearl S. Buck

W-10 **The Battle of Britain,** by Quentin Reynolds

W-11 **The Crusades,** by Anthony West

W-12 **Genghis Khan,** by Harold Lamb

W-13 **Queen Elizabeth and the Spanish Armada,** by Frances Winwar

W-14 **Simon Bolivar,** by Arnold Whitridge

W-15 **The Slave Who Freed Haiti,** by Katharine Scherman

W-16 **The Story of Scotland Yard,** by Laurence Thompson

W-17 **The Life of Saint Patrick,** by Quentin Reynolds

W-18 **The Exploits of Xenophon,** by Geoffrey Household

W-19 **Captain Cook Explores the South Seas,** by Armstrong Sperry

W-20 **Marie Antoinette,** by Bernadine Kielty

W-21 **Shakespeare and the Globe Theatre,** by Anne Terry White

W-22 **The French Foreign Legion,** by Wyatt Blassingame

LANDMARK BOOKS

1 **The Voyages of Christopher Columbus** by Armstrong Sperry
2 **The Landing of the Pilgrims** by James Daugherty
3 **Pocahontas and Captain John Smith** by Marie Lawson
4 **Paul Revere and the Minute Men** by Dorothy Canfield Fisher
5 **Our Independence and the Constitution** by Dorothy Canfield Fisher
6 **The California Gold Rush** by May McNeer
7 **The Pony Express** by Samuel Hopkins Adams
8 **Lee and Grant at Appomattox** by MacKinlay Kantor
9 **The Building of the First Transcontinental Railroad** by Adele Nathan
10 **The Wright Brothers** by Quentin Reynolds
11 **Prehistoric America** by Anne Terry White
12 **The Vikings** by Elizabeth Janeway
13 **The Santa Fe Trail** by Samuel Hopkins Adams
14 **The Story of the U. S. Marines** by George Hunt
15 **The Lewis and Clark Expedition** by Richard L. Neuberger
16 **The Monitor and the Merrimac** by Fletcher Pratt
17 **The Explorations of Père Marquette** by Jim Kjelgaard
18 **The Panama Canal** by Robert Considine
19 **The Pirate Lafitte and the Battle of New Orleans** by Robert Tallant
20 **Custer's Last Stand** by Quentin Reynolds
21 **Daniel Boone** by John Mason Brown
22 **Clipper Ship Days** by John Jennings
23 **Gettysburg** by MacKinlay Kantor
24 **The Louisiana Purchase** by Robert Tallant
25 **Wild Bill Hickok Tames the West** by Stewart Holbrook
26 **Betsy Ross and the Flag** by Jane Mayer
27 **The Conquest of the North and South Poles** by Russell Owen
28 **Ben Franklin of Old Philadelphia** by Margaret Cousins
29 **Trappers and Traders of the Far West** by James Daugherty
30 **Mr. Bell Invents the Telephone** by Katherine Shippen
31 **The Barbary Pirates** by C. S. Forester
32 **Sam Houston, The Tallest Texan** by William Johnson
33 **The Winter at Valley Forge** by Van Wyck Mason
34 **The Erie Canal** by Samuel Hopkins Adams
35 **Thirty Seconds Over Tokyo** by Ted Lawson and Bob Considine
36 **Thomas Jefferson** by Vincent Sheean
37 **The Coming of the Mormons** by Jim Kjelgaard
38 **George Washington Carver** by Anne Terry White
39 **John Paul Jones** by Armstrong Sperry
40 **The First Overland Mail** by Robert Pinkerton
41 **Teddy Roosevelt and the Rough Riders** by Henry Castor
42 **To California by Covered Wagon** by George R. Stewart
43 **Peter Stuyvesant of Old New York** by Anna and Russel Crouse
44 **Lincoln and Douglas** by Regina Z. Kelly
45 **Robert Fulton and the Steamboat** by Ralph Nading Hill
46 **The F. B. I.** by Quentin Reynolds
47 **Dolly Madison** by Jane Mayer
48 **John James Audubon** by Margaret and John Kieran
49 **Hawaii** by Oscar Lewis
50 **War Chief of the Seminoles** by May McNeer
51 **Old Ironsides, The Fighting *Constitution*** by Harry Hansen
52 **The Mississippi Bubble** by Thomas B. Costain
53 **Kit Carson and the Wild Frontier** by Ralph Moody
54 **Robert E. Lee and the Road of Honor** by Hodding Carter
55 **Guadalcanal Diary** by Richard Tregaskis
56 **Commodore Perry and the Opening of Japan** by Ferdinand Kuhn
57 **Davy Crockett** by Stewart Holbrook
58 **Clara Barton, Founder of the American Red Cross** by Helen Dore Boylston
59 **The Story of San Francisco** by Charlotte Jackson
60 **Up the Trail from Texas** by J. Frank Dobie

WORLD
Landmark
BOOKS